TEACHERS FOR THE FUTURE

TEACHERS FOR THE FUTURE

edited by
Victoria Showunmi and Delroy Constantine-Simms

Trentham Books

First published in 1995 by Trentham Books Limited

Trentham Books Limited
Westview House
734 London Road
Oakhill
Stoke-on-Trent
Staffordshire
England ST4 5NP

British Cataloguing in Publication Data
A catalogue record for this book is available from the British Library
ISBN: 1 85856 039 X

Cover photograph by Pablo Mensesawe-Imani

Designed and typeset by Trentham Print Design Ltd., Chester
and printed in Great Britain by BPC Wheatons Ltd., Exeter

Contents

Foreword
Robin Richardson   vii

The Editors and Contributors   xi

Introduction
Delroy Constantine-Simms and Victoria Showunmi   1

SECTION I: Barrier-breakers and Gate-keepers
Chapter 1
The Role of the Black Researcher in Educational Research
Delroy Constantine-Simms   13

Chapter 2
Why Teaching Is Not For Me — perceptions of Black pupils
Shukla Dhingra and Kenneth Dunkwu   35

SECTION II: Obstacles and Restraints
Chapter 3
Teaching for tomorrow, lessons for today
Sally Coulton   59

Chapter 4
'Surely you're imagining things' Black students' experience
Victoria Showunmi   71

SECTION III Supports and Strategies
Chapter 5
The Wise Teacher: The Role of Guidance Workers, Parents,
Schools, Communities and ... Admissions Tutors
Lisa Robinson   89

Chapter 6
The Black Goddess: a perspective on Mentoring
Victoria Showunmi   97

Chapter 7
Encouraging Access: Language Across the ITT Curriculum
Eleftheria Maria Neophytou, Sui-Mee Michelle Chan and   113
Patricia East

SECTION IV Managing effective change
Chapter 8
Raising the Profile of Teaching as a Career in schools and the
community
Amar Khela with Mary Morrison   129

Chapter 9
A Few Timely Sparks: Raising awareness in Teacher Training
Institutions
Mary Morrison with Amar Khela   147

Chapter 10
Recommendations   165

Index   175

Foreword

'The instructor said, Go home and write a page tonight, and let that page come out of you — Then, it will be true.' Thus begins a poem entitled *Theme for English B*, by the African American writer Langston Hughes. The persona in the poem is a 22 year old college student in Harlem. He is the only African American student, he says, in his class.

The student describes his walk after the English B session through Harlem to his digs, and then muses about his own identity. Who and what is he? In what ways is he similar to the other students, all of them white, in his class? In what ways is he different? What has he learnt from them? And what has he learnt from his 'instructor' — the person we on this side of the Atlantic would call tutor or lecturer? What is the relationship between himself and his white instructor, and by extension between himself and the overall education system into which he is growing, and by which he is, he knows, profoundly affected? These are the questions which he raises and on which he reflects.

The poem was written at a time when the word 'colored' was still used by African Americans to describe themselves. 'I guess,' muses the student, 'being colored doesn't make me *not* like the same things other folks like who are different races' — he likes, he says, 'to eat, sleep, drink and be in love' and 'to work, read, learn and understand life'. So the page he writes for English B will not be 'colored', surely? On the other hand, 'being me, it will not be white'. So what, what exactly, is it going to be? This is not, or not only, a question about conventions and preferences in terminology and semantics, but about identity and relationships.

As he wrestles inside himself with this question, the student distinguishes between two separate though interacting issues. On the one hand, there is the relationship between black people and white in American history, culture and politics. On the other, there is the relationship between instructors and students in higher education. In both sets of relationships there are real differences in lived experience which must be acknowledged and respected, not denied. But also in both there is mutuality and inter- dependence: despite differences in influence and access to resources, black people and white belong to each other and cannot escape each other. So do students and instructors. All, regardless of their starting point, and regardless of the fact they do not meet on a level playing field, are affected, are indeed changed and moulded, by the encounters which they have with each other.

'You are white,' says the student addressing his instructor, 'yet a part of me, as I am part of you. That's American.' The insight can be readily applied across the Atlantic, similarly referring to centuries of past history as well as to the present and with the same terse summary of complexity: 'You are part of me, as I am part of you. That's British.'

In common with all other human beings the student likes, he has said, 'to work, read, learn and understand life'. The poem doesn't just say this. Also, it illustrates it. Speaking directly to the instructor who told the students to 'go home and write a page tonight, and let that page come out of you', the student ends his meditation thus:

As I learn from you,
I guess you learn from me —
although you're older — and white —
and somewhat more free.

'This,' he says finally, 'is my page for English B.' The poem is an apposite reflection on the themes of this book, at many different levels. How do children see their teachers, and what role is played in their perceptions by 'race' and ethnicity? How do teachers see children? How do students in higher education in general, and in teacher training in particular, see their tutors and lecturers? How in their turn are they seen? In higher education as in schools how are perceptions, on all sides, affected by notions of race and ethnicity? Many or most educational contexts require the equivalent of 'a page for English B': an assignment, an essay, an examination paper, a research report. When is it appropriate for the lecturer to say, in effect, 'go home and write a page tonight, and let that page come out of you' and when, alternatively, should the requirement be for impersonality and objectivity? Or is the distinction between personal and impersonal writing false, and therefore unhelpful?

These are amongst the questions with which this book wrestles, sometimes entirely explicitly but sometimes also subliminally, between the lines. Throughout there is the assertion that 'you are a part of me, as I am part of you. That's British.' And there is throughout an exploration, therefore, of what this means, and does not mean, in concrete practice.

The book derives from a brave and important initiative by the Higher Education Funding Council in England (HEFCE), which recently helped to set up seventeen separate projects to increase the numbers of black and ethnic minority students in initial teacher training. The book frankly acknowledges and describes some of the inevitable difficulties and problems which the initiative encountered, drawing in particular on the perceptions of those whom it was intended to benefit: black and ethnic minority pupils in schools, and black and ethnic minority student teachers.

Also, significantly, the book draws continually on the perceptions and experiences of black and ethnic minority project workers and researchers. Much of it, not only in this connection but also in others, will be uncomfortable for senior policy-makers and decision-makers, and some at least of its criticisms will appear unfair and unfounded. It will be a pity, however, if senior administrators and academics reading this book are unduly defensive or counter-critical. The HEFCE initiative was worthwhile and is a sound basis for further and renewed efforts. The book will have achieved a valuable aim if it contributes to the endeavours which Langston Hughes outlined as fundamental in all education: 'to work, read, learn and understand life'. I am grateful to have been asked to write this foreword. Just here and just now, this foreword is — as it were — my page for English B.

Robin Richardson
The Runnymede Trust, September 1995

ACKNOWLEDGEMENTS

This book is dedicated to my daughters Chantal and Monique, who have given me the time and space to succeed in the role as editor.

I would like to say thank you to the following:

My family and close friends who have given me support and encouragement throughout.

Gillian Klein who has spent many hours as in-house editor, and as time progressed became a valuable friend.

Robin Richardson, without whose initial support the book would not have been commissioned.

All the Black/ethnic minority students and teachers who took part in the projects, and a special thanks to the teachers who took on the role of mentor.

All the contributors who spent time and energy writing their chapters.

Iris Tapper and Elizabeth Kalio who agreed to share their experiences of the mentor project.

The staff in the faculty of education at Kingston University, especially Linden Langford who spent many hours doing the administration for the project.

My thanks to you all
Victoria Showunmi

I can say without fear of contradiction that the fantastic work of the contributors has made working on this book an experience that I will cherish for the rest of my academic life. More importantly, I would like to express unequivocally to Gillian Klein, on behalf of all the contributors how grateful we are for your guidance, patience, kindness, understanding and all the proof reading you have done. Thanks! I would also like to thank my colleagues at Think Doctor Publications, Alarm Promotions, and Visual Promotions for your loyal support and your honest opinions about my past, present and forthcoming academic projects. I must also thank all the students who participated in the mentor project at The University of Kingston and Victoria O'Lisa of The Windsor Fellowship Trust for their invaluable contribution. A special thanks goes out to Dr Rudy Caine, Dr Rudy Matai, Dr Charles Moody, Dr Stephen Small, Gail Pringle, and my supervisors Dr Colin Samson, and Dr Miriam Gluckman, at the University of Essex, for their academic guidance and of course Brenda Corti, and her staff for helping me with my numerous questionnaires. Finally, I would like to thank my family especially my mum Maud Bennette Anderson (RIP), my father William Constantine-Simms, my stepfather Reginald Anderson, Stephen Anderson, Eunice Smith, Myrtle Bowen, Winston Donaldson, Bobbette Simms, Paul Simms, Beverley Simms, Herman Simms, Morris Simms, Nickell and Renee Simpson, and all their families especially Rashada Latifah Balasal-Simms.

Delroy Constantine-Simms

The Editors and Contributors

Sui-Mee Michelle Chan was born in Cardiff and is of Hong Kong Chinese origin. She was a researcher on the Language and Learning Project at the School of Teaching Studies, University of North London and is currently a researcher at the United Medical and Dental Schools (Guy's and St. Thomas's), London.

Delroy Constantine-Simms is a freelance journalist who has written extensively on issues of race in the British Black press. Currently he is a researcher in education and race at the University of Hertfordshire, while conducting postgraduate research at the University of Essex on Black graduates and equal opportunities policies in employment. He was involved as mentor and research consultant on the HEFCE project at Kingston University. Prior to that he was a teaching assistant in the department of sociology at the University of Stirling, and a tutor counsellor on the D103 foundation course at the Open University.

Sally Coulton is a Black teacher and has been working in multicultural inner city schools since 1989. She was seconded for a year to work on the HEFCE project aimed at widening participation in initial teacher education for people from minority ethnic backgrounds. She is currently working in a Nottingham school as Co-ordinator of Guidance and Support.

Shukla Dhingra is currently working as a trainer in South Notts. College of Further Education in Nottingham. Prior to leading the HEFCE funded project she was the head of ESL service in Sheffield and before that a senior team leader in a similar service in Nottingham- shire. She has served on various local and national committees concerned with equal opportunities and has worked as a trainer in the field of bilingualism and multicultural education. She contributed to an Open University book on Language Diversity and os the evaluator of the EEC funded project on Linguistic Diversity based at the university of Nottingham.

Kenny Dunkwu was born in Nottingham, of Nigerian origin. He is presently working as a researcher at Nottingham Trent University, while completing a Masters degree in education. His main academic interests relate to anti-oppressive education policies, particularly their evaluation and development and he is also involved in voluntary work within the community.

Patricia East is of Irish origin. She is currently Principal Lecturer in Education and Access Co-ordinator in the Faculty of Humanities and Teacher Education, University of North London.

Amar Khela has a wide experience of working in both mainstream and supplementary schools. Posts held include Headship of Punjabi Supplementary School, Director of Storybox Project, Advisory Teacher and Co-ordinator of Bilingualism in Assessment Project. She has been a member of several working parties, an advisor to Yorkshire and Humberside Arts, and an Area Co-ordinator for Kirklees LEA Section 11 projects. During 1993-4 she was seconded to work as a Senior Lecturer and Director of the Teachers for the Future Project at Huddersfield University. She is currently a Project Co-ordinator with the Kirlees MAPs project.

Mary Morrison has worked in a variety of comprehensive schools across the country as an English/Drama/Media and SEN teacher. She was Co-ordinator for the National Oracy Project for the Bradford LEA (1988-91), she now works in Language in Education at the University of Huddersfield, where she wrote the bid and became advisor to the 'Teachers for the Future Project' as Equal Opportunities Officer in the School of Education.

Eleftheria Maria Neophtyou is Greek Cypriot, born in Cyprus and brought up in North London. She was involved in piloting and promoting the work of the ILEA's Language and Literacy Unit, including the work of the Afro-Caribbean Language and Literacy Project. She is currently seconded from City and Islington College to work as Project Leader of the Language and Learning Project at the School of Teaching Studies, University of North London.

Lisa Robinson is a School Liaison Guidance Worker at Thames Valley University, London. She is a member of the National Black Careers Advisers Group [NBCAG] and the African Caribbean Resource and Enterprise Network [ACRE]. She worked with Berry Dicker from October 1993-October 1994 as the Development Officer on the Wolverhampton Project, Pathways to Teacher Training.

Victoria Showunmi lectured in Kent and at Westminster College, where she was Chair of the Gender Committee. She set up a nursery for the children of students at Westminster. Her pioneering work on mentoring students and initiating a positive action taster course for the local Black and Asian community who were interested in teaching as a career led her to the post of researcher in the HEFCE project at Kingston University. She works with her local REC and as a freelance trainer.

Introduction

Delroy Constantine-Simms and Victoria Showunmi

This book explores the under-representation of Black and ethnic minority people in Initial Teacher Training. A series of projects funded by the Higher Education Funding Council has — both overtly and through its hidden curriculum — helped to identify the real barriers that exist. The book doesn't stop there. It shows how educational research on race has itself had negative impact on Black and ethnic minority participation in the teaching profession as a whole.

The book pursues the relationship between school experiences and the psyche of the Black and ethnic minority trainee teachers and describes some of the barriers and problems that these students can and do encounter. There are chapters suggesting practical support systems to ensure that Black and ethnic minority trainees complete the course with as little academic hindrance as possible. Taken together, they provide the foundation for serious debate about the politics of initiatives that endeavour to maintain and improve Black and ethnic minority participation in the teaching profession.

The Background

The Swann Report (1985) notes: 'We regard the under-representation of ethnic minorities in the teaching profession as a matter of great concern which calls for urgent attention. We believe that ethnic minority teachers

1

(and would-be teachers) have been and still are subject to racial prejudice and discrimination'.

Under the Race Relations Act (1976) it is unlawful for an institution providing teacher education to discriminate on racial grounds in the terms on which it admits or refuses admission. It is also unlawful to discriminate in the access provided to any benefits, facilities or services or by refusing to provide goods, facilities or services. The Commission for Racial Equality (CRE) found, however, that teachers were underrepresented in teaching and that almost all were on the lowest rungs of the profession (1989).

At the time of writing, teacher education in Britain is undergoing rapid change. Many Higher Education Institutions (HEI) are forging partnerships and franchises with the Further Education sector, to establish more accessible approaches to admission and entry for students embarking in teaching as a career.

The government has sought to make initial teacher training more school-based and in-service training more school orientated. In November 1993, Education Secretary John Patten announced new criteria for courses of primary initial teacher training. The new requirements applied to all new courses from September 1994 and take full effect from 1996. They affect the subject knowledge, teaching skills needed and the length of training (*Tasc*, 1993). The announcement came at about the same time that Mr Major announced the Government's back to basics campaign.

After the government's new legislation, Black educators sought clarification regarding the Black/ethnic minority agenda among all these changes. The NUT Black Members Conference (1995) urged that school heads give Black teachers greater promotion prospects. They argue that headteachers are ignoring their expertise and giving white colleagues the 'plum jobs'.

One keynote speaker at the conference told the *Voice* (July 4 1995):

> Lack of career progression has long been a bugbear amongst Black teachers. Too many workers have seen themselves work for years, but every time a place on a management course comes up it tends to be White teachers who get sent along. As a result, white teachers are at the top of the queue in being promoted to senior positions.

There has been a sudden spurt of funding aimed at increasing the numbers of Black/ethnic minority students in ITT, and this book analyses some of the outcomes. The Secretary of State's inaugural letter the to Higher Education Funding Council invited the Council to consider how it might, within its funding method or through special initiatives, address the need to widen access. The Council was encouraged in particular to consider how access to higher education for students with special educational needs could be facilitated and to consider the needs of prospective students from ethnic minorities.

The Council agreed, in July 1992, to establish an Advisory Group on Widening Participation (AGWP) to consider and advise it on a range of issues including the two mentioned. When announcing the method for the funding of teaching, in HEFCE Circular 1/92, the Council signalled its intention to set aside a proportion of its funds for teaching to support the Council's polices. The Council agreed that in 1993- 94, £3 million should be made available to improve access for students with special educational needs and £0.5 million for increasing the participation of students from ethnic minorities in teacher education. Its Circular 22/93 spells it out:

> In response to the serious shortage of entrants to teacher training from ethnic minorities, as identified by the Swann Committee in 1985, the second special initiative provides support to projects which aim to increase the participation of ethnic minorities in teacher education.

The Higher Education Funding Council (HEFCE) funded seventeen projects throughout England and Wales aimed at increasing the numbers of Black/ethnic minority students, in what appeared to be an excellent drive towards widening the participation for ethnic minorities within ITT. Interestingly, as each project started to establish itself, a high level of ownership developed, and the members of different projects began to communicate with one another, sharing ideas and information.

Nottingham Trent University took the initiative to write to all seventeen projects and invite them to a meeting where each could describe the aims and objectives of their project. At the first meeting it was decided that there was a definite need for a support group for the people doing the actual work on each project, so each meeting became our support mechanism.

At a later meeting the idea emerged of writing a book from the workers' point of view. We felt that this would be an exciting venture, and would give each project worker the chance to describe their experience. Virtually all the contributors to the book are drawn from the Black/ethnic minority community and it is the Black/ethnic minority voice that gives it such strength. As Black researchers, we were acutely aware of the power dynamics between the project mangers and the project workers, and made it clear at several meetings that the book would be written by the project workers ourselves and the accounts would be presented through our eyes.

This book concerns six of the projects and relates to the aims and objectives set out by and for HEFCE, each chapter highlighting certain aspects. We have included the project titles and a brief summary for readers' interest. They are as follows:

The Projects

Kingston University: Widening Participation for ethnic minority students in teacher training

Aimed to increase the numbers of ethnic minority students entering teacher training. The project carried out both quantitative and qualitative research, to identify the support needs that Black/ethnic minority students may have. A pilot mentor scheme was set up for Black/ethnic minority students who were interested in a career in teaching or already studying in the school of education.

University of West of England Bristol, Faculty of Education: Teaching For Tomorrow Project

Aimed to build on work in the Faculty in order to increase the entry of students from African, African-Caribbean and Asian backgrounds onto courses of initial teacher training, particularly at undergraduate level. The project was conceived as a contribution to deconstructing some of the barriers to educational achievement which currently exist for these groups.

University of Wolverhampton: Pathways to Teaching

Aimed to encourage more young people (14-21 years) from the Black/ethnic minority community to consider initial teacher training. African, Asian and African-Caribbean students went into schools as role models for students of similar backgrounds. The research involved the exploration of the experiences of students on ITT courses at the university.

Nottingham Trent University: Action for Access

Aimed to identify barriers experienced by Asian and African-Caribbean students considering teaching as a career and to develop strategies for attracting more Black teachers into schools and colleges in the East Midlands. The investigation of the existing barriers to teacher recruitment was achieved through formal research undertaken locally.

University of North London: Language and Learning Project

Aimed to provide language and learning workshops for first year bilingual students, including speakers of Caribbean Creole languages, on the BEd and PGCE courses; to monitor the success of the workshops by gathering information from students and their tutors; to provide professional support to tutors working with bilingual students, including staff development sessions; to develop learning and teaching materials to support students' language and professional needs, including a self-study learning pack on the education system in England and Wales, and workshop material.

University of Huddersfield: 'Teachers for the Future' project

Aimed to further race equality in the critical area of the recruitment, education and professional success of ethnic minority citizens within the teaching profession, with the advantages that this will bring to the education of all our children.

Designed to Fail?

The six projects are representative of all seventeen in having clear aims and objectives — which needed to be spelled out if the bid was to be successful. But these aims, however laudable in themselves, were not structurally supported by the HEFCE. In the concluding chapter we make recommendations not only to the HEIs but also to funding bodies, based on the situations revealed in the research described in this book. We also reprint, on pages 159 and 160, the requirements as set out in two HEFCE Circulars, 9/93 and 22/93.

This introduction would be incomplete, and also misleading, if it did not indicate the main areas of failure on the part of HEFCE that strongly affected the course of the projects and their outcome. Among other omissions, HEFCE failed to:

- select institutions that had EO polices in place and demonstrated that these were a) widely disseminated and b) implemented

- establish the status of the newly-appointed project workers
- provide a programme of external monitoring and support
- stipulate a requirement on the part of the HE institutions to demonstrate that changes that the project revealed as necessary would be permanently institutionalised.

This book, then, examines the success and failures of the six projects and makes its recommendations accordingly. It is arranged as follows:

Section One — Barrier-Breakers and Gate-Keepers

This section examines the purposes of research on race and the education of teachers. It highlights the role of the Black researcher and the uses to which it has been put in the educational context. Delroy Constantine-Simms argues that Black researchers are seldom permitted the autonomy they need to manage projects. Kenneth Dunkwu and Shukla Dhingra present an in-depth view of the younger students' perceptions of teacher training as a career option; and give us the voices of the ethnic minority students in ITT and of the qualified teachers, as they speak out about their experiences of teaching training.

Section Two — Obstacles and Restraints

Sally Coulton analyses the 'lessons for today' to be drawn from the project that she co-ordinated — even though she was frequently assumed to be one of the students. And Victoria Showunmi's account of a similar project also in a 'new' university, adds further insights into the dangers of tokenism and the problems of temporary initiatives.

Section Three — Supports and Strategies

This section looks at the types of support available to students while they are in ITT. Lisa Robinson's chapter on the 'wise teacher', explores the role of guidance workers, parents, schools, communities and admission tutors in ITT. She stresses the need for positive action in widening access and making courses more representative to the communities they try to recruit from. Victoria Showunmi reports on the mentoring programme she set up and, along with some of their mentors and mentees in the programme, draws conclusions about what works and why. Eleftheria

Neophtyou, Sui-Mee Chan and Pat East describe the importance of language across the curriculum for students in ITT and illustrate how this supports Black and ethnic minority students — in an HEI with an ongoing programme of support.

Section Four — Managing Effective Change

Amar Khela and Mary Morrison together identify what institutions can do to sustain the initiative that the HEFCE projects were designed to achieve. Amar Khela describes work done in schools to interest young people from ethnic minority backgrounds in teaching, despite their preconceived ideas about the profession. And Mary Morrison identifies seven main areas which the HEIs can make a lasting difference to crucial areas: recruitment and access, interviewing procedures, guidance and networking, curriculum content, school placements and the assessment and monitoring of the progression of students.

The final chapter draws on the findings in the six projects researched in this book and makes detailed recommendations to Higher Education Institutions and to the funding bodies.

The editors and authors of this collection have been motivated by our lived experiences, as educators and researchers, and also by the lack of African and African-Caribbean writers in the field of education. We have taken care to recognise the differences between the specific groups highlighted in the chapters of the book: African, African-Caribbean, Asian and Chinese. One of the motivating factors for compiling and writing this book was to steer readers away from the notion that everyone is the same. Teachers for the future should be quick to question the categories imposed onto African, African-Caribbean, Asian and Chinese people by academics, without reference to how each community sees itself.

Although this book is grounded on sound statistical information and carefully compiled case studies and takes full account of existing published research, its great strength and unique character is derived from its perspective. The white lecturers, administrators and professors who accepted the funding and hosted the seventeen projects saw each initiative from the perspective of the institution — from, in fact, the dominant perspective. Whereas the researchers and project workers saw their work from the perspective of the powerless — the outsiders, the temporary. In this they approximated closely to the perspective of the students themselves. We do more, then, than encourage the students to speak frankly about the prejudice and discrimination they experienced in some of the institutions, over the issue of accommodation and, above all, in the school placements. We reveal also the processes obtaining in Higher Education that, whatever the rhetoric, resist any realignments of power.

Our combined experiences and our insights into the system, as outlined here, present a powerful challenge to the establishment. Token gestures, one-year programmes, rhetoric and opportunist use of funding will effect little change in the long run, as will the present paradigm of research into education and race. If Britain is to attract able Black and ethnic minority members of our society into the profession of teaching, fundamental changes will have to be made in the dominant culture of the educational establishment.

Terminology

AGWP	Advisory Group on Widening Participation
ALLP	African-Caribbean Language and Literacy Project
APL	Accreditation of Prior Learning
ARTEN	Anti-Racist Teacher Education Network, a voluntary network run by teacher educators in the UK which aims to promote equality.
Black/Ethnic Minority	The term Black has been used in different ways in this book. The editors use 'Black and ethnic minority' or 'Black/ethnic minority' as a general term, reserving 'Black' for people of African or African-Caribbean origin. Other contributors, like Dhingra and Dunkwu, use 'Black' as a political term. This use is indicated in the relevant chapters.
CATE	Council for the Accreditation of Teacher Education
CRAC	Careers Researchers Advisory Centre
CRE	Commission for Racial Equality
DES	Department of Education and Science
DFE	Department for Education — since July 1995, Department for Education and Employment

FE	Further Education
HEFCE	Higher Education Funding Council for England
HEI	Higher Education Institution
HMI	Her Majesty's Inspectorate
ILEA	Inner London Education Authority
ITT	Initial Teacher Training
LEA	Local Education Authority
NBCAG	National Black Careers Advisors Group
NFER	National Federation of Educational Research
NUS	National Union of Students
NUT	National Union of Teachers
PGCE	Post Graduate Certificate in Education
SRB	Single Regeneration Budget
TASC	*Teaching as a Career*, a newspaper aimed at educators in the area of ITT
TEC	Technical Education Council
TTA	Teacher Training Agency
UCCA	University for Central Council Admissions
QTS	Qualified Teacher Status

SECTION 1
Barrier-breakers and Gate-keepers

Chapter 1

The Role of the Black Researcher in Educational Research

Delroy Constantine-Simms

In both the USA and UK, Black and ethnic minority researchers assert that white researchers have tended to concentrate on the study of Black people rather than on white racism and institutional racism. The practice continues, as politically left, liberal academics and institutions maintain their academic market by claiming to be the only credible ideological architects on issues of race. This allows them to analyse and recommend their own interpretations of issues as the major ideological components in the construction of an academic platform that serves to create a social environment conducive to bringing about social change.

If this were really the agenda of white left wing academics, then my concerns that the ethnicity and race of researchers does affect research would be totally unfounded. But the true agenda is very different. What white researchers have to face is that, in spite of their willingness to embrace the notion of value-free research, their 'academic objectivity' will itself inevitably be influenced by variables such as culture, value systems, gender, ethnicity and race. Can a white researcher carrying out research on the Black community collect meaningful data on matters related to the Black educational experience, without resorting to the use of stereotypical paradigms as a premise of academic research on race?

Scientific racism and its impact on present educational research

There have been studies on the issue of intelligence and race ever since Binet and Galton applied Darwin's principles of evolution to suggest that there was a biological link between the two. In spite of the flaws in the design, application and use of such data, Hernstein and Murray (1994) have decided to revisit discredited notions to justify their claim that Blacks are less intelligent by virtue of their biological make-up. The previous academic to capture the public and academic imagination on these issues was American psychologist Arthur Jensen, in 1969. He reviewed literature comparing Black and white IQ tests and concluded that Blacks were on average 15 IQ points below the average white population. Hence his claim that educational programmes such as Headstart, geared at inner city African-American children, were a waste of time. Hernstein and Murray (1994) are doing no more than repackaging discredited pseudo-scientific conclusions by right wing academics into 850 pages of so-called scientific research. These authors did not develop their scientific racism in isolation. But IQ studies are not always thus contaminated. Galton (1869) developed the first intelligence test, but the first one to be found useful was developed in France by Alfred Binet and Theodore Simon in 1905. Unlike so many of his contemporaries, Binet appeared to be one of the few early scientists who were prepared to believe that a person's intelligence is not necessarily fixed.

The American psychologist Lewis Terman, of Stanford University, developed Binet's argument and introduced the term IQ as the ratio of Mental age/Chronological age, expressed as a percentage, as outlined in his book *The Measurement of Intelligence* (1916). Terman, unlike Binet, believed that intelligence was fixed and unalterable, along with Henry Goddard, of the Vineland Training School for the feeble-minded in New Jersey and Robert Yerkes of Harvard University. Moreover, they believed that 'inferior' people: paupers, the disabled, and criminals, especially Black people posed a threat to society.

If the hereditarian assertion implied by Murray and Hernstein (1994) were correct, then Black people with some white ancestry and many white genes, should have higher IQs on average than those with little or no white ancestry. Such notions are easily discredited, in studies by Scarr and Weinberg (1977) of the University of Minnesota. They used 43 blood group markers to estimate the proportion of white ancestry of the Philadelphia schoolchildren who were subjects in the study. Since the results showed no association between racial ancestry and four separate tests of intellectual performance, all the correlations being very close to zero, they concluded that there are no associations between race and intelligence.

In Britain, *The National Child Development Study* (1969), revealed that Asian children born in Britain were socially and economically better off than Blacks but not than whites. More importantly, the pattern of IQ scores reflected an almost perfect mirror of the social circumstances of the three groups. Our views are further supported by the findings of the Child Health and Education Study. The children investigated were born in the 1970s and their IQs were measured in 1980. The average IQs of the African-Caribbean, Indian and Pakistani children were found to be 94.3, 95.6, and 90.5 respectively (see Mackintosh and Mascie-Taylor, 1985). These figures suggest that by 1980 Asians were no longer outscoring African-Caribbeans on IQ tests, and this fits with the findings of the study that they were no longer living in socially and economically better circumstances: the Pakistani children were slightly worse off than African-Caribbeans while Indians were marginally better off.

These findings provide powerful evidence against Murray and Hernstein's (1994) claim that race differences in intelligence are determined by genetic factors. They also undermine the claim made by Jensen that environmental factors are inadequate in explaining differences in IQ. In the Child Health and Education Study, a nine point gap was reduced to 2.6 points (Mackintosh and Mascie-Taylor, 1985). More recently a study carried out at Warwick University of more than 6,000 five year olds shatters the myth that African-Caribbean children are trapped from birth by underachievement and low aspirations. Similar results are revealed in National Curriculum tests for seven year olds in English and Mathematics. They prove what African-Caribbean parents have known for a long time: that their children are as bright as or brighter than white children entering the education system but by the time they have gone through that process many are damaged by the low expectations held by some teachers of Black students.

The role of white researchers in race and education research

Many white researchers in the academic fraternity would have you, the reader, believe that their participation in the study of race is of no consequence to the research outcomes since they are committed practitioners of value-free empirical research. A few, however, will admit that research on intelligence and race influenced teachers' expectations of Black people overall. I am concerned that white researchers are continuing to dominate research into race and its dissemination without any real Black researcher participation, beyond that of incidental and ancillary participants, especially in Britain. Given the wealth of negative data that has emerged, I would challenge the claim that race — or for that matter, gender — has had no impact on empirical research.

Discontent with white researchers has been expressed by many a Black researcher, but ignored by white academics and their institutions for decades. White researchers and their academic institutions are forever engaged in politically motivated, policy orientated research on Black people, yet fail to acknowledge that there are fundamental issues of individual and institutional racism in their own backyards which they continue to ignore and consequently do nothing about. I would not be the first to suggest that white researchers would do better to concentrate their efforts on studying the effects of white racism on Black people instead of studying us as part of an ongoing anthropological study for the purposes of economic, political and academic gain. Bourne (1980) asserts that the agenda of certain organisations and the role of certain researchers who work for them are completely misguided:

> It was not Black people who should be examined, but white society; it was not a question of educating Blacks and whites for integration, but of fighting institutional racism; it was not race relations that should be the field of study, but racism (Bourne, 1980).

It is transparently clear that these issues are not just a matter of elementary misunderstandings of research interpretations that can be resolved by rational, impartial discourse. Indeed, she highlights the diametrically antagonistic positions in regard to the cause and nature of racial inequality in the UK, and the political responses which are needed to combat this actuality.

One result has been a proliferation of data that has allowed decision makers to develop policies and practices that virtually condemn Black students as being pathologically unable to learn. Typically, white research has gone relatively unchallenged by Black researchers, because there are not many who are prepared to challenge such constructs. If they try, white academic journals with predominantly white editorial boards appear reluctant to include articles or papers that are incongruent or, worse, challenge their published research findings on the same issues. More importantly, white academics appear reluctant to give any kudos to Black on Black research (with the exception of the Clark and Clark studies), but ardently defend white on Black research, or Black on Black research of the nature of Duncan (1988), who confirms and reinforces their academic expectations of Black children. The critique by Bourne (1980) supports my assertions that white academia has sanctioned and perpetuated pathologies and stereotypes constructed by white researchers; that academia fosters a scenario in which the Black community inadvertently participates as social guinea pigs in the production and maintenance of their own racial oppression and inequality.

The nature of the research of Daniel Moynihan and James Coleman following the 1960s inner city uprising in America provoked similar critiques from numerous Black academics as being 'just another white researcher telling themselves what Blacks already know' (see Billingsley, 1970). In Britain, the debate has persisted well into the 1980s after the Scarman report was published in 1981. This report was rightly challenged in *The Empire Strikes Back* (CCCS, 1982) which questioned the research findings of certain white researchers investigating Black people, who were still offering their academic services to the media as ombudsmen and bastions of knowledge.

The paternalistic approach of many white researchers means white researchers are creating more problems than they are solving, a point fortified by Lawrence (1981) who asserts that race relations sociologists have themselves become a part of the problem of researching race, often under the guise of professionalism and good research dissemination.

Lawrence questions the white researcher's right to be the self-appointed ombudsman. He challenges John Rex and his team at the former SSRC Research Unit on Ethnic Relations, who has consistently maintained that he wishes to use empirical data on racism in society in order to help those who fight against it, and that work on race is underpinned by an explicit commitment to racial equality and justice. Cashmore and Troyna (1981) argue typically in their reply, that Lawrence's stance is an elitist one. It is elitist for white sociologists to continue to enjoy the near monopoly on investigating the Black community, and then representing us in academic journals without our participation or consent.

The most annoying aspect of working with white researchers who look at issues of race, '...is that they automatically become instant experts on race' (Brar, 1992). If Cashmore, Troyna and their supporters looked more carefully at Lawrence's argument they would realise that he was not being elitist by asserting that white researchers are incapable of eliciting meaningful data from Black respondents. All Lawrence does is call into question the validity of the data extracted from Black respondents by non-African researchers, taking account of the views of Parekh (1981) that there are clear power differences between the researcher and the researched and also that there are no common experiences of racism. The lack of shared socialisation and critical life experiences could impair the nature and value of data extracted by white researchers.

A more serious criticism concerns the way in which the data elicited from Black researchers are so often misinterpreted by white researchers. Parekh (1981) argues that white people do not understand the complex structures and behaviours of the Black community:

> ...Most researchers in the field are white. They have no experience of what it means to be Black, and lack intuitive understanding of the complex mental processes and structures of the Black community...

The end product is more white-written research that is ethnocentric and exaggerates the communities' problems that are likely to produce such pathologies, such as identity crisis, negative self-image, inter-generational conflict, unrealistic high aspirations and culture conflict — the very issues that Black researchers are attempting to curtail (see Lawrence, 1982). My analysis of the hidden — but real — agenda of white researchers and the consequences for the Black people researched is that, by bringing Black people into the public eye, government-funded institutions and individual researchers have inadvertently become part of the ideological state apparatus, supplying anthropological data essential for the maintenance of racial inequalities. My concerns are highlighted by Bourne (1980), and Lawrence (1982) of the CCCS collective, who expressed their unease with liberal views thus:

> ...In a situation where state racism has intensified, it is disingenuous for policy oriented researchers to expect that their racist and patriarchal conceptualisations of Black people will not be of interest to the state institutions which oppress Black people. This is not to deny the role of white researchers in the anti-racist struggle; it is to suggest that the principles they avow are in danger of violation when they focus their research projects and programmes on the Black community...

Nevertheless, a provoking question remains: How much systematic evidence of inequality must there be before strategies can be developed to tackle it? The government is not in the business of acknowledging its contradiction on issues of race and ethnicity. As Brar (1992) says:

> ..if taken to the extreme Black research will be marginalised and underfunded, whereas white research on Black people will continue to be seen as important and get more funding.

The role of Black researchers investigating Black issues for white academics

My own experience of research in education and that reported by my colleagues involved in this book, show clearly that it is not we who define the parameters and indeed guide the direction on issues of race. There is little if any participation from the very people who, it is claimed are to be emancipated and empowered. Yet Solomos (1989) argues that, whatever the academic arguments in favour of doing a specific piece of research, it is politically naive and potentially dangerous to see research as separate from its contextual political environment — governments and other interested bodies necessarily take a strong role and have a stake in academic research about so-called deviant groups in society. It would be extremely naive of Black researchers, irrespective of their political persuasion, to believe otherwise.

Moreover, experienced Black researchers are well aware that white academia will continue to conduct research projects without Black participation if they can get away with it. White researchers risk inadvertently giving Black researchers the information required to expose the contradictions of those who publicly articulate liberal ideals, but who privately practice very unliberal actions. The fact of academic life that all Black researchers have to face is that any accusations of racism levelled against white individuals or organisations are received as flawed and invalid. And it does not help when politically unconscious Black researchers are willing to fuel the fire of existing racist pathologies by offering suitable data for white researchers to convey as verifiable fact. As Brar (1992) observes: if you tell a story enough times, an element of it begins to take on a life of its own and inevitably takes on some semblance of dangerous truth. If, for example, we look at the only academic textbook in the field of race and pastoral care, which is written by Carlton Duncan, (1988) a Black headteacher, we can see how he falls into a similar pathology trap when he talks of his Black pupils'...

> natural exuberance, friendliness and sometimes exhibitionist attitude together with their physical appearance (they are often bigger than their peers) are often misunderstood and have earned them such labels as disruptive, antisocial, aggressive...

One has to question the perspective of such authors, especially when they claim that their research is guided by their understanding of what it is like to be Black. Such research makes attacking prevailing pathologies even more difficult: white academics are so keen to embrace these stereotypes and pathologies as endorsed by Black academics, because they reinforce their deep-rooted perceptions of Blacks while vindicating them from any charges of racism.

Clearly, Black researchers have a moral responsibility to expose Black academics who collude with white researchers and academic institutions in the manufacture and marketing of such pathologies as facts. And it is morally imperative that white academics recognise that Black people are not just anthropological research fodder, nor are they political window dressing for academic institutes that claim to be equal opportunities employers. Despite all their political rhetoric about empowering Black people, white liberal academics appear to be the very people who avoid the Black colleagues who are likely to challenge their liberal work by upsetting the academic apple cart which they have filled with their interpretation of the problems surrounding racism and education.

Jeffers (1991) observes that: 'there are many instances within academic research where senior white researchers have employed Black researchers simply in order to get around the issues of access to the Black community': Jeffers describes this as being:

> parachuted in the community. These researchers are often exploited for their ease of access and are at the same time held up as positive examples of positive action equal opportunities policies, while in reality their skills are simply appropriated to further the career chances of white researchers...

In this respect, the differences between academia and other areas of employment are virtually non-existent. In reality Black researchers have very little choice but to watch the white researchers play advocate on behalf of their research subjects and even attempt to become the voice of the powerless by claiming that their research can indeed empower them. Mac an Ghail (1988) claims to empower the researched, but at times slips into the dangerous area of pathologising students, when he the cites Rasta Heads and Sikh Warriors as racialised groups, so perpetuating the myth that all Rasta and Sikh gangs equate with trouble.

Only when Black researchers play an active role in academic research will the production of such pathologies cease. Most Black researchers have at present no mandated positions of authority to influence the outcomes of the investigation or project. Yet I believe that the Black researcher must participate in the dismantling and deconstruction of popular common-sense racist myths by ensuring that in every study the research hypothesis clearly directs research to matters of non-pathological and non-stereotypical concern.

Prominent pathologies that need to be challenged by Black researchers

Black researchers involved in educational research on issues of race are under no illusion about the wealth of information on teachers' racial attitudes. They also recognise that nothing is being done to modify the circumstances that perpetuate these taken for granted perceptions. Are

Black researchers prepared to endorse or collude with existing pathologies in the areas next outlined?

Sports and education

Green (1985) has implied that teachers' presumptions about the academic deficiencies and concomitant sporting prowess of Black pupils is reflected in their strategies, assessment procedures and decisions about setting and option allocations. His research demonstrates how racial attitudes can so influence teacher expectations that they afford differential treatment to Black pupils. Similarly, Carrington (1983), in a study of 11-16 year old African-Caribbean pupils, showed them to be over-represented in sports stream and low level non-academic courses. This study simply reaffirms the racist eugenic assertions regarding Black pupils. The most feasible research hypothesis for white liberal researchers would be to investigate Black students and white to establish whether there is indeed a positive correlation between academic performances and sports for all pupils. If Black researchers investigated Black pupils who had achieved in both sports and academia, this would avoid reaffirming racial stereotypes in the name of white academic research.

Blaming the students

There may be studies about the issue of Black pupils and their propensity to be disruptive and a disciplinary problem, but are there any serious studies that give Black pupils the opportunity to express their opinions about their teacher's expectations? All we have are studies like that of Smith and Tomlinson (1989) who found that the pupils criticised the most did the worst academically. Their study also suggests that girls tended to attract less attention, which probably explains why Black girls are out-performing Black boys academically in school. This conclusion is undoubtedly linked to teacher expectations yet it can take no account of the fact that the blame which affects a child in school is the same blame that is applied to a Black adult beyond the school gates. Gutzmore (1983) identifies the way that the research tradition that views Black youth as a problem gives validity to the criminalisation process and notes that these sociologists include self-claimed radicals.

White teachers' tolerance and intolerance

A crucial piece of research looks at the dynamics between Black pupils and white teachers and shows how teacher attitudes impact on Black pupils, particularly African- Caribbean pupils. Green (1982) looked at six schools (junior and middle). His sample consisted of 70 white teachers and their 1814 pupils of whom 940 were white, 449 of Asian descent and 425 of African-Caribbean descent. Using a Flanders schedule, Green analysed the characteristics of interaction between teachers, boys and girls from each ethnic group. He then invited his teacher respondents to complete an amended version of the British Ethnocentrism Scale. On the basis of these results, he identified two distinct groups: the ethnically highly tolerant teachers and the ethnically highly intolerant teachers. Green's research is summarised in the Swann Report (Chapter 2 Annexe B,) but no mention of it is made in the text of the report.

A comparative analysis of the classroom behaviour of these teachers revealed that the highly intolerant teachers gave African-Caribbean students less positive attention, only minimal praise, more authoritative direction and inhibited their opportunities to initiate contributions to classroom discussions. Green found that the mean self-concept scores of African-Caribbean pupils taught by the highly intolerant were significantly lower than those of their peers taught by highly tolerant teachers.

The challenge for Black researchers is to establish why there are no studies that attempt to investigate how Black pupils felt about the teachers whom they considered highly tolerant or intolerant towards them. Instead we are bombarded with studies which negatively stereotype Black children even before they get to secondary school. Mabey (1981), for instance, found that teachers viewed Caribbean children as young as eight years old as having negative attitudes — a clear reflection of their own attitudes. Black researchers must consider the implications for Black children in the future by investigating whether these so-called negative attitudes are a direct result of negative treatment by white teachers. If, as Green has suggested, teachers' attitudes are translated into classroom action, this is likely to circumscribe the level of educational achievement of Black children. The growing level of discontent with white teachers among Black pupils and vice versa may perpetuate low academic achievement and the increasing vulnerability of Black pupils (particularly Caribbean boys) to exclusion from schools.

Academic performance

Several researchers have labelled Black children as poor academic performers. The data collected by the committee on ethnic differences in examination performance at 16+ and 18+ suggested that in the LEA studied, young people of African-Caribbean descent tended to perform less well than their white or South Asian peers. Data on success in education once again reveals considerable racialised disparities, for example 38% of African-Caribbean men have qualifications beyond CSE and among those relatively few go beyond Ordinary level; the comparable figures for women are 41% and 6% (Brown, 1984: 147). Among the 25-44 age group, 13% of African Caribbean men and 18% of African-Caribbean women had obtained O level qualifications.

ILEA (1987) reported that 93% of the African-Caribbean girls had an average performance of one to four passes compared to 80% of the boys and 87% of white girls and boys. One problem with such figures is that they rarely make a distinction between African- Caribbean and African pupils — white researchers tend to treat Black pupils as a homogeneous group. Nor does it distinguish between the different academic success rates among African pupils. Finally, research figures on academic performances have not explored the criteria used to stream students into certain subjects nor to examine how Black pupils choose their subject options.

Race, class and academic performance

Academic research conducted by white academics in the area of race and education has consistently attempted to undermine Black academic performance by relating it to class and the mediocre success of white working class pupils. Roberts (1981) for example claims that the educational credentials of African-Caribbean school leavers in six working class neighbourhoods were at least comparable to and, in the case of girls, better than those of their white counterparts. In contrast, the research findings of Craft and Craft (1983) in an outer London Borough verify that the examination performance of African Caribbean students was depressed in relation to their white peers from similar backgrounds. Not withstanding the wealth of research data, it difficult to draw any sound conclusions about the impact of race, ethnicity and class on educational outcomes, due to inconsistencies encircling the construction of the research. This is where the Black researcher should attempt to challenge arguments that if one is working class, race is no longer the issue, when there is ample evidence to suggest that it is.

Student teachers' expectations and preferences

The study by Edwards (1978) illustrated how teachers make choices based on unsubstantiated information about pupils they prefer to teach. She presented twenty student teachers with tape-recordings of speakers from different racial and social backgrounds and bi-dialectal people, all British born. There was a working class Barbadian girl who spoke Creole and had a working class Reading accent, an English boy with a working class accent; a Professor's son who spoke received pronunciation (RP), and a recently arrived Jamaican-born girl. The respondents were asked to consider the relative academic credentials of the speakers and their desirability as class members. They behaved as expected. The middle class child was perceived as having the most academic potential and the British born Barbadian girl, when she spoke with a Creole not a Reading accent, the least. Edwards thus exposes the negative preconceptions that teachers have of Black pupils, their accents, and their potential academic ability. Her study demonstrates that teachers assume that pupils with Caribbean accents are low achievers. If and when Black researchers take up this research, they should focus on whether it is racism that encourages the perception of African and African Caribbean pupils as inarticulate and academically wanting, while children with British regional accents, irrespective of the race of the pupil, appear to be perceived as having more academic potential. Black researchers might conduct a study to investigate whether the same perceptions exist about white pupils who have foreign European accents.

Investigation by Figueroa (1986) of images of ethnic minorities held by white students raises further questions. Figueroa administered three questionnaires to a group of PGCE secondary students who attended a short course on multicultural education. The questionnaires were designed to reveal the student teachers' perceptions of and attitudes towards West Indians (sic) and Asians. In common with other studies in the area, Figueroa's encouraged students to articulate stereotypes by completing open-ended statements such as 'When I think about Asians.... when I think about West Indians...' Semantic differential techniques were also used.

Figueroa's previous research had shown that many respondents who were asked to rate white British pupils, West Indian pupils, and Asian pupils, used the 'can't generalise' option, possibly because he, their lecturer, was Black. Yet in his 1986 research, he seemed to be forcing them into a situation where they could do nothing but stereotype. He reports that several respondents nevertheless indicated that they did not want to produce stereotypes. It is surely important to question whether the respondents were afraid of exposing their own prejudices. Other Black researchers could test this hypothesis by asking the same questions as Figueroa, to a similar sample of students teachers, but asking them also where such stereotypes come from and to think about how they could minimise the effects of these perceptions on the pupils themselves.

Research on Black students in further education

More than twice as many ethnic minority young people stay on in full-time education than do white people: for males aged 16-24 the figure was 33% as compared with 11%, and for females in the same group 24% compared with 12% (Skellington et al, 1992: 127). The problem with this data is that it fails to establish why so many Black and ethnic minority youngsters are turning to colleges of further education to continue their studies, be they retakes or A levels. More importantly, such research rarely reveals what happens when the Black students get there and what they leave with. Black researchers need to investigate whether the stereotypical attitudes of white teachers in schools are mirrored in further educational institutes by lecturers and principals. Nothing is said in this type of research about how such pathologies impact on the courses or tutors who select and recruit prospective Black students; nor is there any indication of the courses they study or how successful they are.

However, due to the recent changes in college funding, and the publication of league tables relating to college performance, it is unlikely that any college would allow a Black researcher to investigate the ethnic profile of its students in terms of qualification on entry, course of study, pass rates or failure rates and drop-out rates. To date no institute of further education has provided such data. Yet its provision is important, as it may indicate that colleges of further education also need to have their policies and practices called into question. My reservations about colleges of further education and their ability to equip Black students for higher education are not assuaged by the CNAA, who found in 1987 that only 6% were from ethnic minority groups and that very few of these were Black. If white researchers are interested in tackling the issue of Black academic failure they should look at the issues which perpetuate failure rather than continually reporting it uncritically.

Research on Black students in higher education

In higher education Black students are conspicuous by their absence. In 1990, the PCAS system published its first ethnic breakdown of statistics of UK resident student applicants. A total of 76.7% (131,452) were white, 1.4 % (2,441) Black Caribbean, 1.2% (2,072) Black African and other Black 0.4 (653). These figures are disproportionally low if one considers the higher proportion of young people among the Black population. The UCCA revealed in its first survey of university applicants that only 1% of the university population was made up of all minorities. In addition, research data revealed a high-drop out rate for African-Caribbean students; at least 25% did not take final examinations. The Labour Force Survey (1994) confirms the trend, reporting that 48% of Black and ethnic minority young people now stay on in higher education, compared with a white completion rate of around 97%.

Both these reports are misleading in excluding data regarding foreign students from the Caribbean and Africa. If white researchers really want to investigate the reasons for the continued absence of Black students and their poor success rates, they should look at why Black international students appear to be more successful academically than UK-born Black students. Issues of preferential treatment of foreign students, who pay up to a 100% more in tuition fees than home students, may strongly influence the academic institutions. White academics and educational policy makers appear unwilling to accommodate research which might expose discriminatory recruitment and selection procedures and stereotypical perceptions of Black students abroad and those who are UK residents.

Preventing the perpetuation of pathologies and stereotypes in educational research

Education is a more complex province to research than, say, the biological and physical sciences. In spite of the many useful contributions research has made to education, it fails to provide answers about educational academic inequalities, thus falling short of expectations. An educational researcher has to deal with many variables simultaneously, and some of them may not be controlled or quantified. As my chapter reveals, research is complicated by the interaction between the investigator and their human subjects of study, to the point of influencing the manner in which conclusions are drawn. Such an interaction may even produce changes in the subjects under study.

In the classic division between the researcher and the field of study, a number of principles seem to have wide acceptance: a) the researcher must maintain an objective stance and avoid, as far as possible, approaches which might influence or distort data under scrutiny; b) the search for objectivity is at the centre of all that the researcher tries to achieve, and it helps if events can be reproduced in experimentally contrived conditions. Although objectivity in research is widely accepted as an essential element, the researcher's gender, race, ethnicity, personality, attitudes, beliefs and values might influence their observations of phenomena and assessment of the findings, and consequently can affect generalisations of the results; c) statistical principles should be applied where possible to ensure accuracy and precision in measurement and analysis of data. In the classic experimental design, quantification is seen as a major goal to be pursued.

In recent years a substantial body of social scientists (including educational researchers) have rejected the positivistic approach and the physical sciences model on which it is drawn. They have argued that these principles have little to offer in terms of relevance in the study of complex social situations and human behaviour. Some of them have highlighted the need for qualitative research and analysis of interpersonal structures, and their approaches have been based on quite a different set of assumptions. The following case study is an illustration of this approach.

Case Study
The experiences of Black researchers involved in research supervised by white project managers

A number of my colleagues have found themselves vulnerable to being used by white researchers in a particular way. Black researchers are often in a better position to acquire information from Black subjects than a white researcher. The data is sought with little regard to the needs of either the Black researcher or the subjects. In the words of Roberts (1981):

> Interviewers define the role of the interviewees as subordinates; extracting information is more valued than yielding it; the convention of the interviewer-interviewee hierarchy is a rationalisation of inequality; what is good for interviewers is not necessarily good for interviewees.

We saw evidence of this approach in the project we worked in at a University in south London. The remit of the project was to establish a mentor scheme and carry out academic research to establish what factors encouraged or discouraged Black and ethnic minority students from entering the teaching profession and to gather information on what they thought about their experiences at the University. Following a question- naire distributed to 75 students, 20 students agreed to be interviewed. We, the researchers, like all the students, were of ethnic minority origin; most of us were Black. We empathised with the students and shared the same political agenda and political goals. They were well aware of this commonality of view and felt that the presence of members of the exclusively white faculty at our meetings would be intrusive.

Nonetheless, the staff insisted on participating, with the result that our discussions were inhibited. We soon found that informal gatherings and chats with the students in the canteen and elsewhere were far more useful — and certainly more supportive to the students.

So problems first arose because of the insistence of staff involved in the project on being present at meetings and their eagerness to control the interview process. Their demands were based on a (justifiable) concern that we would be sympathetic to our research subjects and that they might regard us as friends. This, they argued, would distort the data. The possibility of bias distorting data for the opposite reasons was never acknowledged.

The result was that we felt that our wishes and the wishes of the students were overuled. Not only did staff sit in at our meetings but two of the lecturers also wanted to examine the questions we had designed for the interviews with students in their own departments. (The questions were very open-ended.)

We decided to remain true to our agenda and that of the students. When we were asked to hand over the tapes of our interviews, we declined. We did so on the grounds that the students would have been less forthcoming and candid if they knew that their lecturer would hear them, for fear that their remarks would prejudice their academic chances. There was little doubt that some students would be readily identified by their voices or certain things they said.

This claim on the tapes threw us into a huge dilemma. We had to choose between possibly betraying our Black and ethnic minority students — whom we had guaranteed anonymity in the interviews — or risking dismissal from the university ourselves.

We decided to adopt the strategy used by Stenhouse (1985) and discuss the tapes and transcripts of their interviews with the students so that they could check the content for themselves and also decide whether they wanted to disclaim them or withdraw from the project. The Project Manager then claimed (as happened to Stenhouse) that this action could invalidate the research findings. Nevertheless, the education faculty chose later to use this data for their own purposes, so our actions had not been misplaced. The project manager was given access to the modified transcripts on the agreement that she would pay for these — modified — transcripts to be made (my colleague used a Black person not involved with the project to type the transcripts) and that they would remain private to the faculty and be kept in the university archives. She then used these transcripts as part of a staff development training course for the academic staff, which included the lecturers and tutors of some of the students at the time. So only the concealment of the voices, characteristic speech patterns and personally identifiable incidents or remarks ensured that we had, despite the pressures, honoured our promise of anonymity to the students.

As Stenhouse found and we discovered a decade later, such an experience is not uncommon. There is a hard philosophical question here that flies in the face of ethical considerations relating to value-free research and objectivity. For Black researchers working with Black research subjects, it is even more crucial to determine how far the goal of objectivity should be pursued before a stand is taken in the interests of Black people's life chances.

Challenging the perpetuation of pathologies and stereotypes

Research design and preparation

Black researchers should ask the organisation as well as themselves why they are carrying out research in an area in which they already know what the problems and solutions are, and should declare their intention to question any research hypothesis that will inevitably produce negative pathological and stereotypical outcomes before they pursue, or indeed withdraw, from such research. Hypotheses must be developed from a Black perspective. Finally, the important question is whether the problem can realistically be researched other than by Black led research.

The majority of researchers who contributed to this book are involved in collaborative research with teachers, students, schools, government and academic institutions. A major concern for the Black researchers is to ensure that the real purpose and direction of the project is not hijacked by white participants, who also have vested interests in the outcomes. It is up to the Black researchers to ensure that the nature of the contribution of the white people involved is fully resolved, from the point of initial preparation right through to the dissemination of outcomes.

Data Collection

Typically, there is a split between quantitative techniques like longitudinal studies, structured interviewing, systematic observation, and qualitative techniques like participant observation, unstructured interviewing. Much social and educational research, however, uses both qualitative and quantitative methods. Furthermore, studies have combined various sources of data — indeed this is one of the principles of ethnographic research data collection. Black researchers should monitor whether the choices of data collection techniques have been fully explored and how the two methods could be mixed. Within the qualitative tradition there is some disagreement over whether one should develop theories alongside data collection or collect the data first and then look for a link between the data and the theories. Black researchers would argue for the latter, to minimise the contamination of the data by the researcher.

White researchers are very concerned about the validity of qualitative data that is extracted and interpreted by Black researchers. Black

31

researchers are employed because of their ability to access the Black community and extract information in a manner that white researchers cannot. Yet our ability to be objective is continually called into question, and we must defend our stance vehemently. We must also develop the ability to combine data collection and analysis so that we can try out different explanations of the fit between data and theory as we proceed.

Data analysis and evaluation

Have the outcomes of the research been achieved and is the analysis complete, academic and value-free? For Black researchers the area of most importance relates to the underlying assumptions about key concepts and meanings used in the development of past research, because key issues have not been resolved between those who do the labelling and those who are labelled, and those who take on board the label without question or debate. Terminology remains problematic: phrases such as minority ethnic, ethnic minority, people of colour, and Black-British, Black etc. We are seriously concerned about the use of Black to describe Africans and African-Caribbeans as one homogeneous group, or to describe anyone who has experienced oppression. In this I have to disagree even with some of the contributors to this book.

Black researchers must develop skills of cultural academic perception. Academia needs to confront new explanations of events so that new generalisations can be developed about the causes, reasons and processes of behaviour attributed to stereotypes and pathologies relating to Black subjects. The means of analysis depends on the nature of the research design employed and the underlying perceptions, i.e. statistical analysis, class analysis, conversation analysis, qualitative analysis. As Black researchers, it is important to acknowledge problems associated with particular data collection techniques. We must show flexibility by interrogating data bases or Black journals (usually African-American) in the same enthusiastic manner with which we interrogate European sources. There will be problems in terms of gaining such data and also in our ability to use it: the data and sources, combined with our analysis, may be called into question by white researchers on the premise that the data is insufficiently academic.

As stated earlier, moreover, white institutions rarely accept information that will upset the academic apple-cart. Black researchers will need to get onto editorial boards to ensure that their findings are given an equal opportunity to be published and to organise Black forums for dissemination. Unless Black researchers take the initiative, the work on race by Black academics and researchers who want to effect change and bring about social equality will be wasted, or it will merely perpetuate the strangle-hold that non-African and non-African-Caribbean researchers currently have on race related work.

The role of Black researchers in educational research is not to indulge in intellectual gymnastics or to become armchair activists. Unless we Black researchers organise ourselves to challenge the contributions of the Black researchers who are politically naive about issues of race in education, in the same manner that we are challenging white researchers to tackle the racism within their own structures, the perpetuation of pathologies and stereotypes is virtually inevitable.

Bibliography

Billingsley, A.(1970) Black families and white social science, *Journal of Social Issues*, 26, 3, pp. 127-42

Bourne, J. (1980) Cheerleaders and ombudsmen: The Sociology of race in Britain, *Race and Class*, 21. 9,3, pp 3-17

Brar, H.S. (1992) 'Unasked questions, impossible answers' in Leicester, M. and Taylor, P. (eds) *Ethnics, Ethnicity and Education*. London, Kogan Page

Brown, C. (1984) *Black and White Britain: the third PSI survey*. London, Heinemann

Cashmore, E. and Troyna, B. (1981) Just for white boys? Elitism, racism and research, *Multiracial Education*, 10, 1, pp.43-8

Centre for Contemporary Cultural Studies (1982) *The Empire Strikes Back*, London Hutchinson

Craft, M. and Craft, A. (1983) The Participation of ethnic minority pupils in further and higher education. *Educational Research* 25, pp.10-19

Duncan, C (1988) *Pastoral Care: An Antiracist/Multicultural Perspective*, Blackwell, Oxford

Edwards, V.K. (1978) Langauge attitudes and underperformance in West Indian children. *Educational Review*, 30. pp.51-58

Figueroa, P. (1986) Student teachers' images of ethnic minorities: a British case study. Paper presented to World Congress of Sociology, New Delhi 18-22 August.

Finch, J (1986) *Research and Policy: The uses of Qualitative Methods in Social Sciences*, Falmer Lewes

Goulbourne, H. and Lewis Meeks, P. (1993) *Access of Ethnic Minorities to Higher Education in Britian*, Report of a seminar at King's College, Cambridge, University of Warwick Centre for Research in Ethnic Relations, Coventry

Green, P. (1985) 'Multi-ethnic teaching and the pupils' self-concepts' in the Swann Report, *Education for All.* HMSO, London p.46-56

Gutzmore, C. (1983) 'Capital, Black youth and crime', *Race and Class*, 25

Hernstein and Murray (1994) *The Bell Curve: Intelligence and Class Structure in American Life*, Free Press, New York

Jeffers, S. (1991) 'Is race a sign of the times or is it post modernism only skin deep?' in Cross, M and Keith, M (eds) *Racism, the city and the state*, Routledge, London

Labour Force Survey (1994) Ethnic groups and the labour market: analysis from the Spring 1994 Labour Force Survey, *Employment Gazette*, June 1995

Lather, P. (1986) Research as Praxis, *Harvard Educational Review*, 56, 3, pp. 257-77

Lawrence, E. (1981) White sociology, Black struggle, *Multiracial Education*, 9,3,

Lawrence, E. (1982) 'In the abundance of water the fool is thirsty: Sociology and Black 'pathology", in Centre for Contemporary Cultural Studies (1980), *The Empire Strikes Back*, London, Hutchinson

Leicester, M and Taylor, 'The Ethical Problems of Researching Race and Education' in *Ethics Ethnicity and Education.* Kogan Page

Mabey, C. (1981) Black British literacy. *Educational Research* 23, pp.83-95

Mac an Ghail, M (1988) *Young, Gifted and Black*, Open University Press, Milton Keynes.

Mac an Ghail, M (1989) Beyond the white norm: the use of qualitative methods in the study of Black youth's schooling in Britain, *Qualitative Studies in Education*, 2, 3.

Minhas, R, Holland, P, Senn, S, Brah, H. (1988) *Ealing's Dilemma: Implementing Race Equality in Education: Report of the Independent Inquiry into Recruitment and Promotion of Ethnic Minority Teachers in Ealing*, London Borough of Ealing.

Mullard, C. (1985) *Race, Power and Resistance*, London, Routledge and Kegan Paul

Parekh, B (1981) Britain's step-citizens, *New Statesman*, August.

Remmmers, H.H. (1949) The expanding role of research, *North Central Association Quarterly*, 23, 369-76.

Rex, J. (1981) 'Errol Lawrence and the sociology of race relations: An open letter', *Multiracial Education*, 10, 1, pp. 49- 51.

Roberts, H (1981) *Doing Feminist Research*, Routledge, London.

Scarman, Lord (1981) *The Brixton Disorders 10-12 April 1981.* HMSO, London.

Scarr, S. and Weinberg R. A. (1977) Intellectual Similarities Within Families of both Adopted and Biological Children. *Intelligence*, 1, 170-191.

Skellington, R., Morris, P. and Gordon, P. (1992) *Race in Britain today.* Sage, London

Solomos, J . (1989) *Race Relations Research and Social Policy*, ESRC, Swindon

Stenhouse,L (1985) *Active Philosophy in Education and Science*, Allen and Unwin, London.

Chapter 2

Why Teaching Is Not For Me —

perceptions of Black pupils

Shukla Dhingra and Kenneth Dunkwu

Action For Access was set up to develop some strategies for attracting more Black* teachers into schools and colleges in the East Midlands. This Project was funded by the Higher Education Funding Council, the result of a successful bid by the Nottingham Trent University. The Commission for Racial Equality survey published in March, 1988 found that there were not only very few Black teachers (2% of the teaching force compared with 4.4% of the overall population) but that they tended to be on the lowest pay scales and to be disadvantaged in terms of promotion. Ten years on, these concerns are still on the national agenda.

The project wished to investigate the nature of any existing barriers to teacher recruitment in the regional Asian and African-Caribbean communities. To give validity to its initiatives it decided to collect some evidence of the experiences, perceptions and views of Black teachers, students and pupils currently in local educational institutions.

Four questionnaires were designed, each with a specific purpose:

1. to investigate the perceptions of Black and ethnic minority pupils/students in secondary schools and FE colleges to teaching as a career.

2. to investigate the attitudes and perceptions of Black pupils and students taught by Black teachers in local primary and secondary schools. This questionnaire also asked pupils to rate different professions so that we could note the popularity of the teaching profession, in comparison with other careers.

3. to investigate the perceptions of Black teachers currently teaching in primary and secondary schools and FE colleges, concerning their own professional experiences.

4. to investigate the perceptions of Black students in the Faculty of Education, who were undertaking initial teacher training, about their chosen career.

Between December 1993 and March 1994, the team conducted interviews with members of the Asian and African-Caribbean communities. Two questionnaires were directed at pupils and the team completed 96 interviews amongst respondents in primary and secondary schools and FE colleges which had 15% or more ethnic minority students. The total sample taken was 105 students, drawn from four primary, four secondary and four FE colleges, together with the Faculty of Education. The same institutions used to recruit pupil/student respondents were used to contact teachers. Twenty of these teachers were interviewed. All Black teachers in Nottinghamshire were sent a questionnaire and a further 26 replies were received. The total of 46 respondents represents more than half the Black teachers in Nottinghamshire. In addition, a small group of Black students currently studying in the Faculty of Education at the University were interviewed in depth.

Research findings

Questionnaire No 1
To investigate perceptions of Black pupils/students about teaching

The 96 students interviewed were from four secondary schools and four FE colleges. We asked them if they were thinking of pursuing a career in teaching, and, if so, what to do about achieving their ambitions. About one fifth (21%) of those interviewed said that they were indeed thinking of becoming a teacher, twice as many females as males. In terms of what these students were actually going to do about it, slightly over half (55%) of the respondents interested in teaching, said that they were hoping to achieve the required skills and experience and formal qualifications. The remaining interviewees expressed a wish to become a teacher through some other route, for example by teaching outside of the United Kingdom.

The main reasons given by respondents for *not* considering teaching as a career were that they already had another specific career in mind (32%) or because of the nature of the job (28%). A further fifteen percent offered a variety of other reasons such as the perceived low pay, and that they did not want to work with children. Men were slightly more inclined to reject the profession for reasons such as its low appeal whereas women were more likely to rule it out because they wanted to follow another career.

When asked to identify the major influence in their choice of career over a third cited their parents. Another 16% cited their careers officer and 11% said friend(s). Females were more receptive to official sources of influence, such as their teachers/lecturer, or careers officers. Almost a fifth said that they would be largely influenced in the choice of career by some other source, in most cased themselves, but they also named historical and political leaders such as Martin Luther King and Malcolm X.

In reply to the question: 'What might encourage you to choose a career in teaching?' almost one fifth (19%) mentioned the presence of more Black teachers as role models. About 15%, mainly men, thought that better pay would attract more Black teachers and a tenth saw the opportunity to improve the academic achievement of Black pupils as a motivating factor. A quarter of those replying gave a variety of other answers relating to the

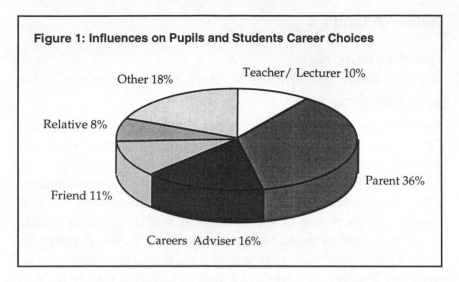

Figure 1: Influences on Pupils and Students Career Choices

Other 18%

Teacher/ Lecturer 10%

Relative 8%

Friend 11%

Parent 36%

Careers Adviser 16%

availability of all-Black schools, more control over children and the possibility of teaching subjects not currently on the curriculum.

Other data collected relates to the people who influence career choices. The pie chart (Fig. 1) summarises the responses given by the school and FE college pupils and students to the question 'Who will be the major influence on your career'?

Questionnaire No. 2
To investigate perceptions of Black pupils/students towards Black teachers within primary and secondary and schools

The graph (Fig.2) indicates the pupils' responses to the question: What is the effect of having a Black teacher in school?'

Further analysis revealed some differences between the ethnic minority groups. African and African-Caribbean children were more likely to say that it was easier to relate to Black teachers and that they received more help from them. Furthermore, they suggested that Black teachers had a greater understanding of the problems caused by racism than white teachers. Although Asian respondents agreed with this view they were more likely to answer in terms of ethnic minority staff being role models or an inspiration. It is worth noting that Asian respondents thought that the presence of ethnic minority teachers would help to eliminate racism. Female students in particular thought that having teachers from the same

Fig: 2

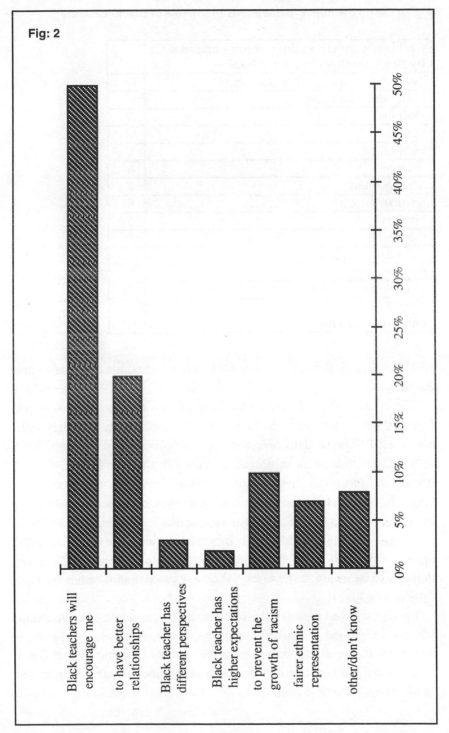

Fig. 3: charts the pupils' perceptions of the role of Black teachers

Children's understandings of roles undertaken by Black teachers in their school	%
Teacher (no specified specialism)	17
Community Languages	15
Helper	12
Sport	12
Humanities	8
Science	8
Management	7
English	6
History	6
Counsellor	5
Substitute Teacher	3
Support Staff	3
European Language	2
Technical Subject	2
Other/Do not know	31

ethnic background made it easier for teacher and pupils to relate to one another.

The young people described the type of jobs they considered Black teachers were most likely to carry out in schools. Note that they only identified 17% as actually teaching. This is because some students have only taken into account subject areas in which they are taught, such as history or humanities. If one adds to this all the mentions given to the specialist subject areas then the role of active teacher is in fact mentioned by 64% of respondents. So the majority of Black teachers are seen to do just that — teach. It should be remembered that this set of results is based upon the perceptions of the pupils and students. The respondents are unlikely to be aware of the teachers' actual status, and whether they are full- or part-time.

Pupils may well perceive the remaining 36% as doing some teaching but saw their prime responsibilities as in other areas such as management and pastoral care. It is apparent from the results of the survey that Black teachers are not concentrated into a small number of subject areas but work across the whole curriculum.

Pupils' perceptions of problems faced by Black teachers

Children were asked in the survey to describe problems they believed Black teachers would face in their school. Their responses are summarised in Fig. 4

Fig: 4

Perceived problems	Rank
racism from pupils	1
isolation	2
racism from staff	3
lack of respect	4
relationship problems	5
other/do not know	6
lack of promotion	7
skills and abilities undermined	8
tokenism	9

There were four key problems: racism from pupils (38%); isolation (19%) racism from staff (17%) and lack of respect (15%). There were some differences between how African-Caribbean and Asian students saw matters. Racism can manifest itself in many forms and individual targets of racism may perceive or think of it in different ways. Asians were more likely to think of teachers suffering racism from pupils, whereas African-Caribbean students tended to think in terms of the lack of respect shown to Black teachers; and of racism from members of staff and problem of isolationism.

Pupils' perceptions of a range of careers

The pupils were asked to reveal something of their attitudes to various professions, by rating them in terms of importance. Their responses are summarised in Fig.5.

The profession receiving the highest ratings were, in descending order, doctor (66%), lawyer (58%), teacher (48%), hairdresser (25%) and plumber (24%) were rated the lowest.

Respondents of African-Caribbean origin tended to rate the police as a profession lower than Asians did, but were more likely to rate hairdressing as a important career. Asian students rated the profession of lawyer more highly that African-Caribbean students did.

Figs: 5 and 6

Profession	Very Important	Quite Important	Average	Not very important	Not important
Teacher	48	33	15	2	2
Electrician	18	27	28	19	8
Police Officer	48	17	18	8	8
Nurse	45	32	13	8	2
Hairdresser	7	15	26	27	25
Lawyer	58	25	8	5	5
Social Worker	46	34	10	7	3
Plumber	11	11	30	24	24
Doctor	66	19	10	1	3
Mechanic	19	28	30	14	9
Bank Manager	25	37	24	8	5

Female	Male
58%	42%

Ethnicity and Gender of pupils in survey group

Asian	African Caribbean	Mixed Race	Other ethnic origin
54%	36%	2%	6%

Traditional 'male' trades such as electrician and plumber were more highly rated by males than by females, although this was not true for hairdressing, which was more highly rated by male than by female interviewees. Fig. 6 illustrates the ethnic composition of the sample of pupils surveyed.

Questionnaire No.3

To investigate perceptions of Black teachers currently teaching in primary and secondary schools and FE colleges

A questionnaire was sent by post to all Black teachers — approximately 80 currently working in the county. A total of 46 ethnic minority teachers took part in this survey, of whom twenty were interviewed individually. Fig. 7 illustrates their routes into teaching. Most qualified by means of a Post Graduate Certificate, closely followed by B.Ed degrees and Cert. Ed.

Fig 7 Respondents Routes into Teaching (%)

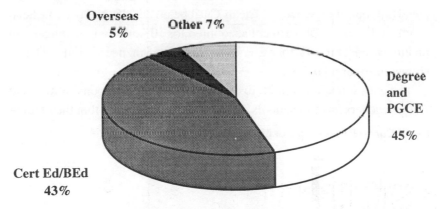

The teachers interviewed were asked to give their reasons for entering teaching. The two most popular reasons by far were that it had been a lifelong ambition and that they enjoyed working with children. Interestingly, two respondents said that the reason they had entered teaching was because their parents had been teachers.

The respondents told us how long they had been in their latest school and what their current position is (see Fig. 8 below). A large majority (64%) had been in their present school for five years or less. One quarter (24%) had been in their present school for 6-10 years and 7% for 11-15

Fig.8: Respondents' Length of Time in Current School

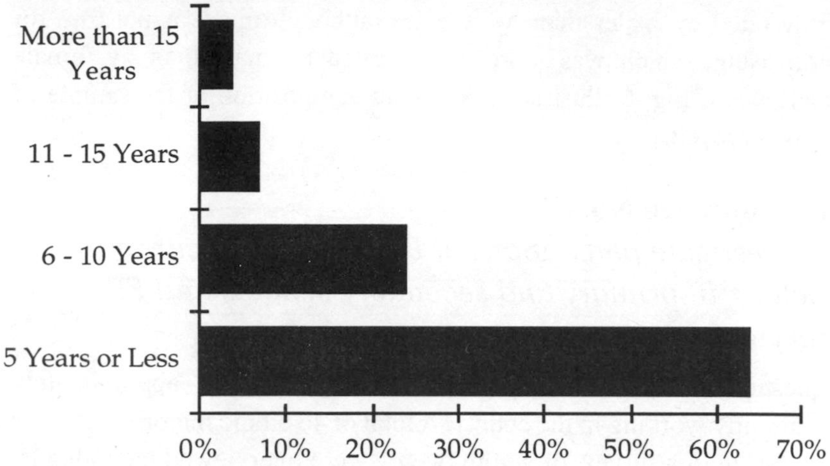

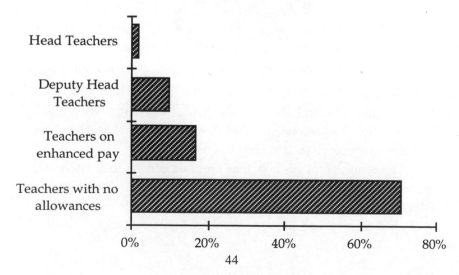

years. Only a very small number (4.5%) had been in their present school for more than fifteen years.

The greatest number of those interviewed (71%) were unpromoted teachers. One tenth of respondents had achieved the position of Deputy Head (all four of these were African-Caribbean) and 2% had become head teachers. Heads of Department accounted for 10%, those in management positions 5% and a further 2% were on other enhanced points. This is shown in Figure 9 below.

The questionnaire went on to examine the type of responsibilities that Black teachers have in schools. Just under one-third said that they taught

Fig 9: Current Teaching Position (%)

Fig. 10

Responsibilities of Respondents	%
Specialist subject	28
Tutors	24
Management	17
Policies	17
Class	17
Home Liaison	13
Pastoral Care	11
Staff Development	7
Multicultural issues	6
Counselling	4
Budget	4
Special Needs	4
Support teaching	4
English to parents	2
Other	33

their specialist subject, while another quarter said that they were tutors. The other main areas of responsibility identified were home liaison, pastoral care, and management policies. The full range of responsibilities undertaken by Black teachers is shown in Fig. 10.

The teachers interviewed gave their reasons for entering the profession. The most popular was that the individual had always wanted to be a teacher (31%), followed closely by enjoyment of working with children (24%). Just over a tenth (11%) had parents who were or had been teachers and this had encouraged them to become teachers themselves. Other reasons given included encouragement by their own teachers, that it was a high status profession outside the UK, that it was good work experience, and that they had enjoyed school as a pupil.

Female respondents were much more likely to enter the teaching profession because they had always wanted to be a teacher or because they had enjoyed working with children. Males were more likely than females to have come to the profession from another career. African-Caribbean teachers were more likely wheras their Asian counterparts were more likely to express a liking for working with children.

A proportionally higher number of African-Caribbean respondents said that they aspired to a headship, just under one third of the men and one-quarter of the women interviewed. Almost half the women interviewed aspired to a higher scale for their job, and when asked how they planned to achieve their aspirations just under half said that they would start by improving their management skills. Men were much less likely to answer in this way although it is not possible to say why. Could it be that they do not rate the possession of management skills as highly or do they feel that they have already such skills?

The teachers were also asked to relate some of their experiences in schools. Over a third (35%) of Asian and a quarter (25%) of African-Caribbean respondents had encountered some form of overt racism. The two respondents in the 'mixed race' or 'other' categories had also suffered racism. Thirteen percent felt that they were not valued and approximately one tenth (11%) felt alienated. Both Asian and African-Caribbean teachers felt that they could relate to the students and parents of ethnic minority community groups more effectively than their white counterparts. Proportionally more African-Caribbean teachers felt that they acted as a role model for pupils.

Respondents were then asked 'Why do you think there are so few Black teachers in education?' and their replies are shown below in Fig. 11.

The two main reasons cited were the negative experiences to which they had been exposed as Black pupils, and the perceived poor promotional prospects (10% each). Female respondents gave three main reasons: poor promotional prospects, lack of role models, and racism shown towards teachers.

Lack of Black role models and low pay were also given as key reasons, closely followed by lack of careers advice and the underachievement of Black pupils. Racism towards Black teachers was cited by 7% of respondents and the same percentage quoted parental influence. Parental influence was more important amongst Asian respondents, whose parents considered teaching to be a relatively low paid/low status profession.

Fig. 11 and Fig. 12
Ethnicity and Gender of Teachers in the sample group (Fig 12).

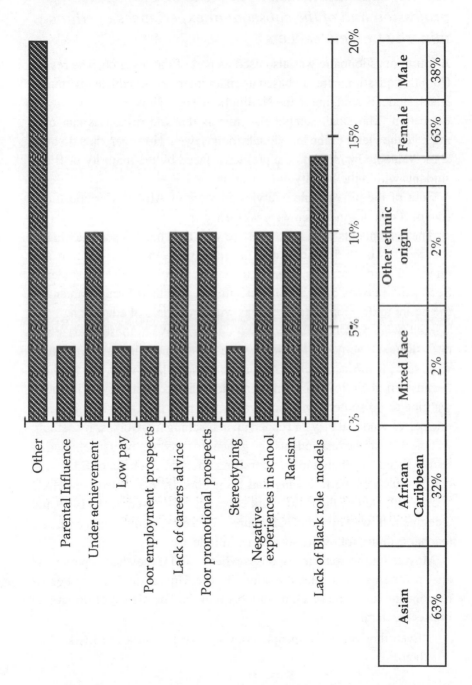

Questionnaire No. 4

To investigate the decisions made to enter the teaching profession and of the subsequent experiences of ethnic minority trained teachers

A fourth questionnaire was also used as part of the research. The results from this questionnaire are based upon an interview conducted with nine Black students studying at the Nottingham Trent University's Faculty of Education. The small sample size means that the responses can only indicate the views of the individuals interviewed. However, they do offer some valuable insight into the problems faced by the majority of Black students within the Faculty of Education.

Four of the nine people interviewed were of African-Caribbean and five of Asian origin. Seven were women.

The respondents were asked to state why they had chosen teaching as a career. Two-thirds said that it had always been their ambition and one-third said that they wanted to act as a role model to students. Secondary reasons included disillusionment with their former career and the desire to develop their own ideas within the field of education.

And *'what factors influenced your choice?'* Five of those interviewed cited the need for more Black teachers and the same number said that they were seeking job satisfaction. A couple of respondents went into teaching because of their love for children and other reasons given included wanting to do something which was better than their previous job, and one person said that they had ended up in teaching more or less by default.

One third of the respondents had gone into teaching by first completing their 'O' and 'A' levels and then enrolling upon the Bachelor of Education course. Each of the following had been done by one person: an HND course followed by the B.Ed, work experience followed by the B.Ed and a degree followed by the PGCE course. Two other people had come into teacher training following some time in industry.

Most telling were their responses when asked if they had experienced any problems as a Black person in the University. A number of respondents identified lack of support and the prevalence of direct and indirect racism.

> 'Even though 'white' people copy my work I get lower marks than them.'

'Assumption by some lecturers that just because you're Asian you are from India.'

'I was called a 'Black bastard' whilst on teaching practice in a predominately white school.'

Lack of knowledge and awareness about ethnic minority cultures on the part of the white teaching staff had led to some stereotyping of the ethnic minority students. Only one student claimed to have experienced no overt racism in the university.

Four out of the nine people interviewed suggested that greater emphasis should be placed on multicultural education. Two respondents felt that more emotional support ought to be made available for Black students. Other suggestions were the appointment of more Black lecturers and the further promotion of equal opportunities. One of the interviewees was very pleased with the current level of support at the university and the provisions for Black students.

Finally, the respondents were asked to suggest how the recruitment and retention of Black teachers in training could be improved. Five said that more Black teachers were needed to promote teaching as a career. Three said that more positive images of Black teachers were required and several students suggested that the teaching profession should improve its advertising campaigns. It was also suggested that more should be done to strengthen links between ethnic minority communities and the teaching profession, including the recruitment of more ethnic minority governors into schools.

Cogent Comments

We can gain further insights from what the students said. These are some of the remarks made by Black pupils about why they would not choose teaching as a career:

'Teachers get no respect. You have to be careful how you teach because pupils don't listen to teachers.'

'Not a nice role at all, pay seems low, and you can't go up the ladder with this job.'

'There are a lot of hindrances, being a Black person prevents you from having that authority in the classroom.'

When Black students in the survey were asked: 'What problems, if any, do you think Black teachers face in this school?' the responses were strongly worded. Some students described the impact of racism in its overt forms:

'Racism — got rid of a teacher in the school who said f...off paki'.

'being Black put him in a spot where other students could say anything to him.'

Other Black students, however, saw the racism in their particular institution as taking a more covert form:

'Racism from students, teachers — they would often talk behind his back.'

'Other teachers segregate themselves from the Black teacher. He often feels the odd one out.'

'There's so much racial discrimination, you see it all the time.'

'Due to racism there are a lot of Black teachers unemployed.'

'There are not a lot of Black people in teaching and a lot of people put them down.'

Many of the Black pupils and students interviewed within the study had low expectations of their ability to achieve the academic qualifications required to enter teaching, as the following statements illustrate.

'I would go for teaching if I could get the grades.'

'I would be encouraged by seeing more Black teachers, there is a lack of role model incentive'

'I have another career in mind — electrician.'

Over a third of respondents (36%) said that the biggest influence on their choice of future career was their *parents*. Often parental preferences for certain jobs were affected by socio- economic factors or cultural traditions, as research by Ballard and Veillins (1986) showed:

parents encourage and pressure their children to do well and refuse to be fatalistic about failure. Socialisation at home puts a high evaluation on discipline and hard work and, should children fail to 'clear' an examination, they will be encouraged to take it again and again until they do.

Careers teachers, however, seemed to see things differently. Some students reported a lack of appropriate guidance and positive encouragement from careers teachers, with the result that they did not consider teaching as a potential option. One said that the Careers Officer has not mentioned BEd and the students considered that this was covert racism.

The Black and ethnic minority pupils interviewed were clear about what they saw as the key problems for Black teachers, namely racism from pupils, isolation, racism from staff and lack of respect. They said things like:

'Whites think he's got the job because of his skin colour, not because of his ability.'

'In a class, if you have a Black teacher, there are divisions in a class.'

'White children would pick on the Black teacher and not value his opinion.'

'They're not respected as Black teachers. White teachers outnumber Blacks, so they often feel isolated.'

Black pupils and students commented upon the racism which staff encountered from white colleagues. They spoke about:

'Isolation and intimidation from some white teachers.'

'Lack of respect shown to him by white teachers and students.'

They were in no doubt, however, about the advantages to themselves, the Black pupils and students, of having a Black teacher, as their statements show:

'Black teachers always understand me; they can teach us about our culture.'

'Having a Black teacher made me work more and think about teaching.'

'Seeing Asians in different positions and you think YEAH!'

The Black teachers themselves saw the absence of role models and the poor promotional prospects as potential barriers to entering the teaching profession. In the words of one teacher:

'Black people don't see many Blacks, so they think the profession isn't for them. If you see a lot of Black people in a profession then it inspires you to go into that profession.'

Many Black teachers interviewed stated that they were automatically being pigeon-holed as experts on multicultural issues. This kind of 'de-skilling' created an image of them as 'professional ethnics' rather than as teachers who brought particular cultural skills and a broad range of experiences.

The majority (92% of the Black teachers interviewed) had been in teaching for more than five years, and were not being promoted at the same rate as their white colleagues. These are some of their comments:

'Since I started this job in a secondary school ten years ago, my teaching status has remained the same...promotion is hard to come by.'

'...valued only in relation to ethnic minority issues.'

'At times I feel that my abilities have been overlooked in favour of others.'

'Career opportunities are limited.'

More women than men teachers interviewed identified racism as part of their personal experience in the education system.

'Assumption that you're not a true representative of the African-Caribbean community because you are successful.'

'Racism is present throughout the education system. It is present in the attitudes of many colleagues, parents and children.'

Students on initial teacher training at Nottingham Trent University also identified racism as part of their experience but some said they had not been subjected to overt racism. The following comments are typical:

'Teachers making jokes of Black students.'

'There is no definition of what is a racist comment and what isn't.'

'In my teaching practice I experienced racism, especially in all white schools.'

Conclusions

The Action for Access Project was not alone in finding that amongst the wide-ranging difficulties cited by the teachers, experiences of racism, lack of promotion, and isolation appeared to stand out. (CRE, 1988, Siraj-Blatchford, 1991 Singh, 1992). In Modood's 1994 report *Ethnic Minorities and Higher Education,* he reveals that some universities may be directly or indirectly discriminating against ethnic minority candidates. His study is based on research into more than 500,000 entrants to higher education in 1992. The results confirmed for the first time that 'variations in ethnic groups' entry to higher education cannot wholly be explained by differences in performance at school'.

When higher education authorities started to collect data on ethnic minorities, the ethnic disproportions were already known. University for Central Council Admissions (UCCA) said that this was not due to discrimination but could be explained if one looked at additional factors: ethnic minority students apply disproportionately for highly competitive courses such as medicine and law and not for lower level courses such as teacher training, so they are less likely to be successful; ethnic minority candidates do have lower A-level scores and are more likely to resit their A-levels; finally, they tend to apply to local institutions, which also limits their chances. But the report disputes these commonly held assumptions. UCCA fails to explain why Pakistani and Caribbean origin students, with A-level grades identical to successful white candidates, are less likely to gain admission to universities. However, in spite of these problems, it was encouraging to note that one fifth of the students interviewed in the Action for Access Project were interested in taking up teaching as a career, simply because they 'just wanted to be teachers' or they 'love children' or want 'to be role models for Black children.'

So the question is 'will these students ever see the inside of an initial teacher training institution? If the answer is to be 'yes', institutions will have to develop action strategies. We suggest what these might be, based directly on our research findings: the needs expressed by Black teachers, students and community groups, and the discussion held with staff and students in University. There are four areas which will need to be developed.

1. *Outreach Work*

- Reach out to ethnic minority community organisations, including youth groups and women's associations, to disseminate information on teaching as a career.

- Develop a clear framework of activities, including promotional talks, displays and exhibitions featuring Black teachers working in schools and colleges.

- Provide more comprehensive guidance interviews to potential applicants, informing them about entry qualifications and courses available for teacher training.

2. *Promotional Material*

- Positive images of Asian and African-Caribbean communities should be reflected in the University's brochures, course booklets, posters and leaflets. The main text of posters and leaflets should be written in two or three local community languages.

- Information on routes into teaching should be simplified and written in a more user friendly language.

- The ethnic minority press should be used extensively for advertisements and information about 'Teaching as a Career'.

- Profiles of school and college students interested in entering the profession should be prepared and work-shadowing experience organised for them in other local schools.

3. *Closer Links with FE Colleges and Schools*

A two-fold pro-active approach is recommended to develop closer links with local schools and colleges, particularly those with a high proportion of ethnic minority students, by:

- participating in careers conventions and special days organised by secondary schools and colleges to provide information to students on teaching as a career.

- Encouraging schools and FE colleges to participate with Compacts in teacher training.

4. Support for Black Students within the ITT institution

- by development of a Black student support group.

- by raising awareness of all students of the University's equal opportunities policies and relevant laws such as the Race Relations Act and the Children Act.

- By giving more explicit information on complaints procedures regarding racism and discriminatory institutional practices.

- Setting targets for appointment of Black staff, in order to provide role models for students.

- Setting targets for appointment of Black staff, in order to provide role models for students.

- to meet the specific needs of students, a particular requirement should be the appointment of Black counsellors. A national shortage of such counsellors means that unless opportunities for on-the-job training are provided, this problem cannot be adequately addressed. It is possible to get exemption (Section 5(2)d. Race Relations Act) for training and this should be pursued.

One of the most challenging tasks for teacher training institutions lies in changing the negative perceptions of teaching amongst ethnic minority groups. However, what is needed most is a high level of institutional commitment, to ensuring that any step taken includes rather than excludes people from the Asian and African Caribbean communities in the UK.

Note

* Although the editors of this book use the term 'Black' specifically to demote people of African and African-Caribbean origin, the authors of this chapter use terms as follows:

    Asian — people whose ethnic origin is from India, Pakistan, Bangladesh, China, other Asian groups.

    African-Caribbean — people whose ethnic origin is from Africa or Caribbean

    Black — Generic term for all of the above and to include people of mixed parentage

    Ethnic Minority — all of the above

Bibliography

Ballard, R. and Veillins, S. (1985) South Asian Entrants to British Universities: a comparative note, *New Community,* Vol.IV, No.3, 325-336c

Commission For Racial Equality (1988) *Ethnic Minority School Teachers. A Supplementary Survey of Eight Local Education Authorities,* CRE London

Department of Education And Science (1985) *Increasing The Supply Of Ethnic Minority Teachers,* A Consultative Paper Circular No.1, Further Education Unit

Singh, R. (1988) *Asian and White Perceptions of the Teaching Profession,* Bradford and IIkley Community College

Modood, T. (1994) 'Undergraduates Face Unfair Selection', by Kausar Butt in *The Weekly Journal Newspaper* Issue: 123 pp3 Sept 8th 1994.

Siraj-Blatchford I (1991) 'A study of Black Students' Perceptions of Racism in Initial Teacher Education. *British Educational Research Journal,* Vol.17, No.1 pp.35-50

Department of Education and Science (1985) *Education For All;* Report of the Committee of Inquiry into the Education of Children from Ethnic Minority Groups, HMSO, London (Swann Report)

SECTION II
Obstacles and Restraints

Chapter 3

Teaching for tomorrow, lessons for today

Sally Coulton

Preface

This chapter attempts to draw comparisons between the experiences of Black people in secondary schools, at university and in the community. It examines the role played by educational institutions in perpetuating the under-representation of particular ethnic minority groups in initial teacher training (ITT) and tries to identify ways in which this can be tackled. The term Black in this chapter refers specifically to people of African-Caribbean and African heritage, although other political, social and cultural meanings that can be applied to this term are acknowledged.

Introduction

The experiences which young people gain during their education have an immeasurable impact on them throughout their adult lives. Research by Mac an Ghaill (1988), Gillborn (1990) and Mirza (1992) illustrates that young Black people are getting a raw deal from the British education system. Wright's (1986) study of two multicultural secondary schools found a conflictual relationship between 'Afro-Caribbean' pupils and their teachers in both schools, and she suggests that this led to these pupils being placed in lower ability bands. Wright's findings are echoed in my experience of supporting these pupils in schools where they are disproportionately represented both in the exclusion statistics and the 'non-academic' classes in certain subject areas. It seems likely that this situation will continue unless strong action is taken by those who have the power to make changes.

Taking responsibility — the role of the school

While working across a number of secondary schools it has become clear to me that teaching staff have a fundamental responsibility to ensure that the educational experience of all pupils is largely a positive one. However, there is a great deal of evidence from research and from personal testimony which suggests that for many Black pupils schooling is an unfavourable experience that does little to value their culture and identity.

As an advisory teacher supporting pupils of African-Caribbean heritage, I was able to see at first hand the conflict that existed between these pupils and some of their teachers. This situation was exemplified by the way in which certain African-Caribbean boys were perceived, particularly by white male teachers, who considered them to be generally more aggressive and challenging than their white counterparts. So it is hardly surprising that these young people do not identify with teachers, and moreover, have little interest in entering Higher Education (HE) and becoming teachers themselves.

In addition to behaviour management issues, schools also perceive that there is a problem of under-achievement, which seemingly prevents Black pupils from realising their potential. If we subscribe to the notion that Black pupils are under-achieving, we must, therefore, assume that certain expectations of these pupils already exist amongst teaching staff. Bird et al (1992) carried out a study for the Department of Employment to identify ways of widening access to HE for Black people. Much of this work focused on school liaison and how effective links could be developed between schools and HE. From interviews with Black pupils it became evident that they perceived low expectations of them to exist in the minds of both teaching and guidance staff.

Many of the negative experiences of Black pupils in schools are connected to institutional discrimination and government policies, such as the eurocentric National Curriculum. However, there are indications that individual personnel have an influential role in changing the attitudes and expectations of young Black people. Teaching staff who are viewed as supportive by Black pupils are often those who have a greater awareness of the cultural backgrounds of these pupils, and who are prepared to listen to them and enable them to share their culture and feel valued.

I ran a group for boys of African- Caribbean heritage in one secondary school where I was based. It took time to get this group off the ground due to the scepticism of some teachers about the purpose of initiating such a group. During group sessions it became apparent that these pupils relished the opportunity to express their views about what it was like to be a Black pupil in the school. The boys had a clear perception of their academic and social status. They were also aware of the negative views of some staff about the existence of the group and cited this as further evidence of racism.

The huge divide between the ideology of these pupils and that of their teachers was, and I believe still is, one of the major factors contributing to the under-representation of Black people in the teaching profession.

The HE experience — the work of the project

The experience of working in secondary schools provided me with the motivation and interest to co-ordinate one of the HEFCE projects, which was designed to increase the recruitment of minority ethnic students into ITE. I realised that this was an area that urgently needed to be addressed and considered that my background would enable me to do this effectively. I had not anticipated the transitional difficulties I would encounter in moving from school to a Higher Education Institution (HEI).

As a Black teacher I felt quite comfortable in a school environment where Black pupils constituted between twenty and thirty per cent of the school population. I was able to formulate positive working relationships with staff and parents, where issues of ethnicity were given a high profile. I also felt a sense of belonging where I could work alongside others who shared my cultural heritage.

The Faculty of Education where the HEFCE project was based was part of a new university which occupied a satellite site in an affluent area of the city, where there were few minority ethnic occupants. On moving into the Faculty the sense of belonging which I had felt in school vanished rapidly. My new environment was almost exclusively monocultural, the prevailing culture being white European. I had expected this to be the case amongst the staff, as it often is in school, but in the Faculty this dominant ethnic background also extended to the students. This was my first impression of HE and it will be a lasting one, one no doubt also experienced by the very students the project was trying to attract into the Faculty.

I joined the Faculty at a turbulent time both politically and organisationally. The Faculty was being managed in an interim way pending the appointment of a new Dean, and was anticipating a reduction in its student allocation, as a result of government policy. The implications of this unfolded during the first term of the project. It took a considerable amount of time for Faculty staff not directly involved in the project to know who I was and what I was doing there. Their assumption that I was a student did however give me a useful insight into the way in which students are treated by some Faculty members.

The constraints of the project time scale were immediately apparent. One year in which to begin addressing some of the barriers to teaching which exist for people from minority ethnic backgrounds was unrealistic, particularly as the project was concerned with raising aspirations and challenging attitudes. Initially the only official staff contact I had was with my line manager but as the limitations of this structure became clear, a steering group was formed.

One of the principle difficulties I faced in developing the work of the project was in establishing an effective mechanism for identifying, and subsequently involving, Black students in the project's activities. My work with school pupils had served to highlight the importance of using appropriate personnel whom pupils could relate to and therefore any work to be undertaken with schools needed to adopt this approach.

An estimated three per cent of Faculty students came from non-white backgrounds, but there were no official channels through which to contact them. I particularly wanted to make contact with some of the small number of African-Caribbean and Asian students in the Faculty, as these groups were the ones most significantly represented in the local school population and recruitment from these communities was to be the focus of the project.

I raised the difficulties of making contact with Black students with the steering group, and this caused a great deal of debate, ending in a lack of solutions and much despondency on my part. I had plans to undertake a variety of activities with these students, such as creating a support group, making a video and initiating a mentoring scheme. The issue of contact permeated all the intended work of the project and I was unsure how the problem could be resolved.

The Faculty had a policy on the monitoring of ethnicity whereby the students' declaration of ethnic status during registration was optional, and little work had been done by the University to persuade students of the positive reasons for ethnic monitoring. Some steering group members considered it unacceptable for me to contact students on the basis of their ethnic background, and the consensus was that students should approach me to participate in the project rather than my taking the initiative.

A conference that I attended with some other project researchers and co-ordinators helped me to consider how best to move forward with the project. I learned that my situation was far from unique and that the difficulties I was facing were common. The striking feature of these difficulties was that they were being experienced mainly by Black staff in majority white institutions and this made me question the commitment of such institutions to take on the issues that were integral to the success of the projects.

Black student teachers — issues and concerns

Once I finally made contact with Black students in the Faculty, I set about explaining the objectives of the project and how the students might take part. As the project progressed, certain constraints seemed to prevent Black students from becoming fully involved. These related to the nature of ITT courses and the difficulties already faced by many of the Black students in the Faculty.

ITT courses require students to spend a significant amount of time in school and so out of the Faculty. Many of the African-Caribbean and Asian students in the Faculty were mature students with additional responsibilities, who did not have the time to take on extra activities such as mentoring. Financial hardship meant that some students had to seek part-time employment and this further curtailed their participation in the project. More importantly however, some of these students were experiencing difficulties with their programmes of study and involving them in the project could mean burdening an already overloaded group of students with yet more responsibility without first providing an adequate framework of support.

During informal discussions with these students certain areas of concern were identified about aspects of Faculty practice. The most widely expressed were to do with:

- eurocentric programmes of study which reflected the National Curriculum and did little to recognise and value the contribution made by those other than of white European backgrounds
- the criteria for selection of block school experience placements, which left some students feeling isolated as the only Black person in the school
- a lack of awareness by some staff and students of issues pertaining to the cultural identity of Black students. A Hindu student cited as an example that Religious Education was delivered through worksheets rather than utilising the expertise and experience of the students from various religious and cultural backgrounds
- the perceived absence of an effective support structure, where students could discuss issues of 'race'

These issues were highlighted in an interim report prepared for HEFCE, about the work of the project. The report was brought to the attention of the steering group and the initial reaction from Faculty staff was fairly defensive. I felt myself to be in the uncomfortable position of having the validity of the report questioned. That the views expressed in the report pertained to only a minority of students served to reinforce the sense of marginalisation that appeared to exist for them and myself.

The Faculty had a system whereby personal tutors were assigned to all students, to provide support and guidance throughout the course. The majority of Black students that I interviewed did not see this system as particularly relevant to them and many said that they could not relate easily to their tutor. They welcomed being able to talk with a Black member of staff and felt confident to discuss issues of ethnicity. These discussions also provided me with a support network and reinforced my sense of identity. Fundamental concerns, such as the provision of support for Black staff in the Faculty, are not discussed in this chapter but they should certainly be included as part of any future supportive framework.

The Black students reported some particularly worrying incidents, incidents which might be indicative of the progress that needs to be made by the Faculty in recognising the needs of these students. A Muslim student told me that her tutor, who was male, insisted on telephoning her at home, despite her explicit request that he did not do so, because her parents found it unacceptable. She also complained that the Faculty did not recognise the need for her to be given a block school experience placement that allowed her to continue living at home. It was only after considerable effort on her part that this request was granted.

An African Caribbean student on block school experience in a white rural area about 100 miles from the Faculty had expressed some concern about the attitude of his Head of Department, who was, he felt, discriminating against him. He was told that other students had not had any difficulties with this teacher, insinuating that he was at fault. This left him feeling extremely isolated and unsupported. He subsequently failed his placement.

These incidents serve to illustrate the way in which institutions often fail to put equal opportunities policy into practice. Further, they emphasise the need for regular evaluation and assessment of the effectiveness of provision for Black students. Without a comprehensive system of monitoring the success (or otherwise) of these students, HEIs cannot hope to make informed decisions about the best way to meet their needs. The Faculty in question has taken steps to address this issue and is looking to improve upon its present practice.

The current position regarding the responsibility of the school in the training of student teachers means HEIs need to ensure, within their partnership agreements with schools, that there is provision to support Black students and address relevant issues. It is clear from the experiences of the Black students involved in the project that some placement schools had not considered the implications of receiving Black students. The new role of teachers in ITE means that substantial professional development will be needed to enable them to effectively support Black students during their school placement. Consequently, this raises the question, 'who will provide this training for teachers?' Surely not the HEIs who have yet to 'get it right' themselves.

Working with the community — attracting Black students

Part of the work of the project was to develop strategies to assist in increasing the recruitment of Black students into the Faculty. Initial Teacher Education does not seem to be a particularly popular course for people from minority ethnic groups. This is indicated by the continuing need to recruit from these groups (resulting in the HEFCE initiative), and the disproportionately low number of Black student teachers in the faculty where the project was based. In developing links with a variety of groups that serve the local Black community, I attempted to determine the factors that prevented or discouraged Black people from becoming teachers.

Through informal meetings and information sessions I was able to identify a number of factors inimical to the progression of African-Caribbean and Asian people into HE and teacher training. These factors come as no surprise and are explored in greater detail elsewhere in this book. They include:

- a lack of knowledge about the range of opportunities available in HE and of the existence of Access courses for those without formal qualifications.

- Asian heritage people who had qualifications gained in their home country but not recognised in Britain, requiring them to undertake a further four year course.

- the financial constraints of being a student and the commitment needed to sustain the period of training

However, the most significant factor for many Black people seemed to be:

- the negative view they had of the education system, which related directly to their own experiences or those of others close to them.

The latter point exemplifies the way in which personal and institutional discrimination in the education system impinges upon the lives of Black people, long after they have left it.

In this social climate it becomes difficult to envisage ways in which HE, and particularly teaching, might be viewed positively by Black people. A starting point may well be to try and bridge the gap that currently exists regarding the culture of ITT and that of the communities which it is trying to attract. In focusing promotional activities toward the Black community, HEIs must ensure that both their personnel and the resources used are appropriate and relevant. It would seem that there is still much work to be done by faculties such as the one in which the project was based, to develop links with community groups.

The HEFCE project may have been instrumental in assisting the Faculty to establish contact with these groups. Nevertheless, maintaining this contact without the services of a full time co-ordinator will require a level of motivation and commitment which I doubt exists at present in the Faculty or elsewhere in HE.

Outcomes — the way forward

The most successful outcome of the project was the production of promotional materials which could be used by schools, colleges and the community. A video was made illustrating the experiences of some of the Black students in the Faculty, and showing them at work on school placement. The video was launched to local teachers and community groups together with Faculty staff and was very positively received.

The strength of the film seems to be its realism, where the students provide the narrative through interviews, answering questions relating specifically to their experience as Black teachers. A typical incident is recounted by a student who was on placement in a village school in a rural area. The Black student was attached to the reception class. On the first day in the school, one of the pupils asked a white student in the group: 'Are you all teachers?' She replied, 'yes', to which the child, who was about five years old, responded, 'what, even the Black one?' This incident serves as a reminder of the attitudes that prevail in society, preventing Black people from achieving all they are capable of. It is hoped that the video will serve as a catalyst for continued work with the Black community and raise awareness within the Faculty and outside of it about the experience of Black students and teachers.

The Black students who participated in the video felt that they elicited a great deal of curiosity and questioning by the pupils, especially if they were placed in a predominantly white school. They perceived the existence of stereotypical attitudes about Black people in both playground and staffroom. This was not acknowledged by the teaching staff in the programmes of study in the Faculty or by staff encountered on their school-based experiences. Many of the issues raised by the video are emotive and some powerful messages are conveyed to those currently responsible for the provision of teacher education, in both schools and HEIs. These issues relate particularly to the extent to which educational institutions recognise that Black students may have specific experiences and needs which are not addressed within existing ITT courses.

Summary

The cyclical model of disadvantage may begin with Black children's negative experience of schooling, which impedes academic achievement. They see few positive images of people from their cultural background with whom they can identify and may become disaffected with education. The conflictual relationships which some young Black people have with their teachers serves to reinforce negative attitudes toward education, attitudes which can prevent future involvement in further study. Those who are able to progress within the education system and enter higher education, find themselves in a marginal position. Those who decide to become teachers are further disenfranchised and seem more likely to experience difficulties during their training than other students.

Throughout the education system, Black people are working against mechanisms obstructive to their achievement. There is obviously some way to go before teacher education is seen as an attractive and viable option for Black people. By identifying the barriers that presently exist for potential students, we may be able to devise more effective ways of providing support. However, it must be recognised that discrimination is inherent within the education system and those involved in the delivery of education at all levels have a responsibility for tackling it.

References

Books and articles

Widening Access to Higher Education for 'Black People, London, Department for Employment 1992

Coulton, S. (1994) *Teaching for Tomorrow — interim project report for HEFCE* (unpublished) UWE, Bristol Faculty of Education

Gillborn, D. (1990) *'Race', Ethnicity and Education, Teaching and Learning in Multi-Ethnic Schools*, London, Unwin Hyman Ltd

Mac an Ghaill, M. (1988) *Young, Gifted and Black: Student-Teacher relations in the schooling of Black youth*, Milton Keynes Open University Press

Mirza, H. (1992) *Young Female and Black*, London, Routledge

Siraj-Blatchford, I. (ed) (1993) *'Race', Gender and the Education of Teachers*, Open University Press

Verma , G. (ed) (1993) *Inequality and Teacher Education: An International Perspective*, Lewes, Falmer Press

Wright, C. (1987) 'Black Students — White Teachers' in Troyna, B. *Racial Inequality in Education*, London, Tavistock

Video

Coulton, S. *Black to the Future: Teaching as a Career*, UWE, Bristol, Faculty of Education 1994

Chapter 4

'Surely you're imagining things'
Black students' experience

Victoria Showunmi

Introduction

As teacher training is being wrenched from the hands of the established ITT institutions into schools, we need to be aware of what Black and Asian students are experiencing while studying on full or part time ITT courses. Evidence shows that many of these students are still up against barriers which can and do affect their learning. As educators, we know that the students' experience is what the whole process is supposed to be about; it is the *raison d'être* of both the individual staff and the institutions themselves (Haselgrove, 1994). Such a view is confirmed by the arbiters of quality in Higher Education. Teaching, Learning and the Student Experience is one of the nine major categories in the outlined checklist for auditors (HEQC, 1993:14). Of the 119 topics in the *aides-memoire* for Assessors, 57 relate directly to students' experiences (HEFCE, 1993: 26-8).

However it is clear from a review of the literature e.g. (*HE Abstracts* Vol. 23) that the providers of HE are interested predominantly in one segment of students' experience — their role as learners. With the academic support of the Higher Education Funding Council for England and the Higher Education Quality Council, students' views were sought about the performance of staff in the facilitation of their learning experience. How do Higher Education Institutions (HEI) respond to the students' voices?

As researchers at a new university in south London, working on a HEFCE funded project to attract more Black and ethnic minority students into the teaching profession, we found that little account had been taken of earlier research into, and descriptions of, such students' experiences while undergoing their training. All the problems identified in the earlier studies were still being encountered by these students in 1994. So this research could only conclude that, so far, the students' voices continue to go disregarded or unheard.

Their concerns had less to do with purely academic issues that with conditions and circumstances they faced that made their experiences significantly more difficult than for their white colleagues. Several of the students were convinced that the main reason they had been given places at the university was to increase the numbers of Black and ethnic minority students in the faculty of education.

Accommodation

Our research revealed that the most painful experiences for Black and ethnic minority students generally concerned accommodation and placement in schools. Sensitivity and foresight on the part of the university could have alleviated if not wholly prevented, some of the difficulties the students had to face. This lack of planning was compounded by leaving the students to deal with the problems themselves.

> I have experienced looking for accommodation in university. The accommodation I found was close to the course itself that I'm on. I found alternative accommodation to where I was, and again tried the university area for a while and I just kept getting negative responses, so I gave that a dismissal and I looked for alternative accommodation and found accommodation with Black people. The Black community which has been helpful to me. (student 3)

Many HEIs have embarked on million-pound building schemes without asking what students might want from their accommodation services. Because of their focus, which is mainly on the learners' perspective, HEI make strategic decisions which take little account of the rest of the students' lives. Iram Siraj-Blatchford (1991) suggests that Black students need support from their student services to help with difficulties over accommodation and quotes one of the students in her study:

> The student houses are well mixed. Houses either had majority of 'home/white' students or a majority of 'Black/overseas' which led to incredible ghettoisation and stereotyping of each group. There is no relationship with the wider community, it's very isolated and this has led many students into feelings of misery (p.42).

It would be true to say that both the UK educational researchers and HEI have taken little interest in matters outside of learning that influence the student's experience. The USA model suggests more enthusiasm on focusing on the whole person. For example, Pascarella and Terenzinis (1991), reviewing how college affects students, focus on the outcomes for students, including cognitive skills, psychosocial changes, attitudes and values, moral development — as well as the more familiar territory of career choice. Institutions only began to be concerned with individuals in a more holistic manner as applicants rather than as students when they were threatened with the demographic downturn. This prompted HEI, individually and collectively, to explore different student markets, in particular mature, often female applicants who were not coming from the hitherto typical school-leaver background.

Since such students were taken up, their attributes, behaviour and performance has been the subject of research investigations (e.g. Fulton, 1989). I would argue that this interest stems from the fact that non-traditional students were different from school leavers and challenged HEI with the notion that their experience enriched the learning process. The reality is that their HE experience derives from their roles other than that of the learner alone. It is clear that non-traditional-entry students have 'difficulties' with HE because of what is happening in the rest of their lives. This might be financial, emotional or to do with racism. The effect of such issues on the student's learning process has pushed the matter higher onto the agenda in HEIs. If one stands back, one will see that these areas have always impinged on students' experience of Higher Education. The ethos in the university under discussion, however, did not permit such discussion.

The Swann Report (1985) observed that teacher education has confused two distinct forms of 'multicultural education': to prepare students to teach in a multi-racial school or to teach in a more homogeneous school but in multicultural society — but neither really grasps the nettle. Cohen (1989), among others, acknowledges (and regrets) the existence of student teachers who are racially prejudiced. Students from Cohen's study expressed genuine concern lest they themselves exhibit unintended prejudice, and a belief that teachers need to be selected in respect of certain characteristics, not least, that they should be free from prejudice.

The Student and the Parameters of Knowledge

Much has been written about the eurocentric and indeed nationalistic nature of the school National Curriculum. However, the notion of a prescribed body of knowledge, Western-defined although frequently not Western generated (eg. the zero in mathematics or the base of 10) permeates all the HE institutions of the UK. Students in the university under discussion themselves argued that there should be opportunities on the course to explore the ways in which knowledge, as constructed and structured, contributes to the legitimating of inequalities and oppression. The existence of a hierarchy of subjects and the prescribed content of each is, the students argued, itself circumscribed by patriarchy and the dominant cultural values.

This level of critical thinking is to be welcomed and nourished but the students felt that staff treated such questioning as a problem. Yet if there is to be fundamental change, all students (and lecturers) need to be equipped with the intellectual skills to examine critically the nature of the curriculum so that, as teachers, they can evaluate and challenge the ideologies that underpin the National Curriculum. There is a pedagogical as well as a curriculum content here, too, and it relates to both school and HEI learning. In the words of Nigel Wright:

> Once we stop thinking of knowledge as a thing to be put into learners, like liquid to be poured into jugs, and start thinking of it as something created by each learner for himself or herself, the implications... are far reaching.

The Student and the Establishment

The overt interpersonal aspects of racism suggest that policy-makers need to address the issue of racial harassment. Education for democracy implies the full participation of all groups, including Black/ethnic minority groups and this demands the exploration of shared values. Despite concerns over racism in education, the failure of schools to meet the needs of Black/Asian pupils and calls for more Black/Asian teachers to be employed, the number of Black/ethnic minority students recruited into teaching remains low. The evidence, notably from the UK Commission for Racial Equality (CRE), suggests that their career prospects are often poor. Similarly, the University of Michigan survey carried out between 1966 and 1978 showed a 60% decline in the numbers of Black students selecting education as a major. In 1987, in the entire state of Michigan, only eleven Black male teachers under the age of 27 were certified to teach. According to a survey released in 1988 by the American Association of Colleges for Teacher Education, less than 10 percent of the students in a typical college of education are members of minority groups (Moody, 1988).

Some of the barriers that students are facing are identified in this book. Firstly, one needs to understand the ethos of ITTIs and what they stand for: that initial teacher training institutions are fundamentally different to mainstream HE. When asked about their ITT institution, most students will describe it as an extension of school. The surroundings and the kind of interactions that take place between student and tutors regarding their chosen study programme highlights the differences from other HE centres. Students who enter university through the traditional route appear to fit into the ethos of ITTIs more readily than Black/ethnic minority students.

Access is the first step in the cycle of increasing Black participation in Higher education. However, the university must first work to improve the image or perception that Black people have of them. The commonly-held view is that there is a lack of commitment to equity in the recruitment of Black students and the employment of Black faculty and staff. More attention is thought to be given to legalistic action and bureaucratic paperwork than to real increases in enrolment and employment equity (Moody, 1995). Being open and honest with students about the curriculum, the accommodation, and the experiences of other Black students is vital. Another possible answer could be the extreme pressure that student teachers find themselves under. One student explains some of the pressures experienced while trying to complete the course:

> Being a mature student, with children and trying to cope with the pressures of university and still holding onto the role of mother and wife. Sometimes, it feels that every day is stress related. (student 7)

One of the barriers to the achievement of Black students, faculty and staff is the expectations held of them by the majority group. Expectations not only determine students' outcomes but is also the quality and quantity of our interactions with students. Teacher Expectation and Student Achievement programmes (Kerman, 1974) allow us to observe some common classroom behaviours that directly correlate to student achievement:

- How often do we call on Black students?
- How long do we wait for Black students to respond?
- How many prompts or cues do we give Black students?
- Do we acknowledge Black students' responses?
- Do we acknowledge Black students as human beings?
- How close do we get to Black students during the teaching and learning process?

The ease with which many educators are able to discount, devalue and dismiss what Black students bring to the institution is another major barrier to their success. These educators are exercising, and abusing, their enormous power — the power to define the terms. It is they who define whether or not something is mainstream or marginal (Moody, 1995).

Policy responses

Clara Connolly (1992) claims that in this increasingly competitive climate, there is inevitably mounting pressure for procedures and practices within institutions to be more effective, more clearly spelt out, and for institutions to be held more accountable for their polices. An Equal Opportunities policy has the advantage of being recognised and supported by law. Legislation exists to prevent discrimination and to allow for positive action to correct injustices. Higher Education Intuitions, in particular, ought to have developed a framework for recognising the seriousness of equal opportunities for both students and staff. The most plausible argument for preferential treatment for past wrongful injuries relies upon the very principle of equal opportunities (Boxill, 1991). According to Boxill, this principle is based upon the notion that positions in society should be distributed on the basis of fair competition among individuals. Higher education in the past may have been perceived as preparing ten per cent of the population for higher positions in society.

However, more opportunities through access for students and the value placed on education itself, suggest that the issue is about much more than just fair competition. In times of scarcity and unemployment, access to higher education becomes a double-edged sword. Access allows entry into higher education for those who have been disadvantaged, but may not take into account financial hardship, crowded teaching, poor accommodation and eventually graduate unemployment (Henry et al., 1992). Equal opportunities is seen as a means to achieving an end, but not as an end in itself. However, the principle of respect for persons is central and underpins any policy of equal opportunities in that persons are valued for themselves.

Black/Asian students may experience a sense of helplessness or loss of personal autonomy because of unfair treatment, if the policy of equal opportunities is incoherent or inadequate. For example, if abuse of power and role occurs through the unequal relationship that exists between student and lecturer then positive action ought to be taken to correct the injustice. Or the student may be treated disrespectfully, which may in turn, affect their levels of performance. Although some institutions have a separate harassment policy, the issue itself comes under the umbrella of equal opportunities.

Harassment is also a recognised a feature of discrimination, one which requires a sensitive approach. A policy is useful because it involves principles of fairness and justice (Henry et al., 1992). The next step brings us to the area of students' charters. Charters involve guidelines for good practice and the identification of standards, and should reach a wide audience and reaffirm fundamental principles and values. However, difficulties can arise: if a charter is imposed upon a group of people without a sense of ownership by all concerned, then the charter could be impossible to use as a guideline and have little sense or meaning. There is a need therefore to identify shared principles and values before compiling such a document. New charters and codes often arise when there is a lack of consensus about the values within a society, and particularly in times of dynamic change.

The National Union of Students' (NUS) Student Charter clearly outlines the basic principles of accountability to students, and ITTIs should take cognisance. When institutions operate under the assumption that they can somehow attract traditionally underrepresented students by merely waiving admission requirements, without providing support services vital to such students successfully completing their chosen academic path, whatever their claims of providing access they are, in reality, limiting traditionally underrepresented Black students' participation to selective academic concentrations (P. Rudy Mattai, 1995).

Black teachers' own experiences of schooling

Black students' experiences of school and the attitudes of teachers towards their Black students have been well documented, providing us with evidence of the ways in which schools serve to limit the life chances of many Black students (Wright, 1986, Mac an Ghaill, 1988, Bansal, 1990 and Mirza, 1992). The students taking part in the HEFCE studies were, on the whole, those who had managed to survive their schooling and had achieved examination results which gave access to higher education. A smaller number had left school without the necessary formal qualifications and had come into higher education as mature students by circuitous routes. Many Black students re-live some of their past experiences when they first return to education. Some of these experiences are still very much alive and if the student is not given support, their past experience can act as a great inhibitor of success:

> I think it was the education system, I mean very early on, I got the impression that I wasn't very bright, I got that from the teachers. They gave you the image that you develop of yourself, it is primarily them, and I felt that I wasn't very good, I wasn't very bright and it wasn't until I grew up and was an adult and did various different things that I realised, that well I'm not quite that thick, that I am brighter than maybe I think I am. I feel resentful for that. I feel that I have wasted a lot of years simply because I lacked the confidence. That I'm fairly bitter about. (student 7)

> I find myself, personally, that I'm a Black person and conscious of being Black and aware of what happens to Black people and am all the time challenging simply because I find tremendous stereotype assumptions in education, whether it is in literature, whether it is in the way Black people walk, the way that Black people are perceived and to me that is what education is about. (student 3)

The CRE publication *Learning in Terror* (1987) describes some of the effects of racial harassment on the everyday life of Black children. Racism is always damaging in an educational context. It can undermine self-esteem (Milner, 1983) and often leads to resistance and consequent under-achievement (Wright, 1986). The effects of direct and indirect racism from teachers and lecturers are especially menacing: their assessments of the students' work are more than likely to be affected.

Why a career in teaching?

A survey of students' perceptions of teaching as a career (Singh et al., 1988) noted a marked similarity between the views of South Asian and white respondents over discipline problems and poor promotion prospects, but the presence of racism among pupils and teachers was a significant point of difference. Asian respondents identified it as among the least attractive aspects of teaching, whereas whites either disagreed with this view or 'did not know'. In the present studies, racism was a highly visible theme running through most of the students' comments, yet although many remembered incidents in their own schooling which had been particularly painful, this was not always explicitly developed in the students' accounts: most often it was taken as given, a routine experience and one of the realities of daily life. Some students expressed a concern that racism might hinder their progress in teaching, but most were determined that they would overcome such difficulties. For a small number of students, the recognition of the inadequacies of their own schooling was the primary motivating factoring in choosing teaching as a career:

> I just feel that if I had a better education prior to coming here, I wouldn't have had to work so hard to get myself up to standard. I wouldn't have had to put in the amount of hours that I've had to put in. Having said that I mean, my expectations myself are very high,

but I still feel, when I started the course, I didn't feel that I was prepared academically. (student 7)

'Black teachers would provide motivation and in turn be a role model. I would be more aware and sensitive of the difficulties Black/Asian students go through coming from the same background. (student 4)

An HMI report, (DES, 1989b) responding to the concern about the under-representation of ethnic minorities in the teaching profession expressed in the Swann Report, suggested that the presence of students from ethnic minority backgrounds is helpful in raising awareness of diversity and in establishing the normality of that diversity: 'They can make a particular contribution in seminars and workshops' (DES, 1989b: 19). There is a fundamental danger in this approach: ITTs could lean on Black students as being their 'professional ethnics' (Blair and Maylor, 1993), experts in Black culture, rather than treating them as individuals with a full range of experience and knowledge:

It feels as students you have to belong to the elite group of professionals and to fit in you have to think and act like them... (student 1)

Every school I have been to has been virtually white, everyone has been good to me. I have worn Indian suits, taken Indian sweets, shown Indian dances, and talked about Divali and tried to fit in... I was scared at first, that they were going to make fun of me but it was OK. (student 2)

We had to read this book in English, I was like the only Black person in the class. It was an English and Drama group on Tuesday and we were split into groups, because of the size, we were put into groups A and B. It so happens that I was the only Black pupil in A and we were reading this book and we were told to voice our opinions. I said what I had to say and the white pupils gave me looks with daggers. It wasn't exactly what they said, it was how they said it, but that came across. The discussion was about this girl who is mixed race and the father died and the mother could not look after her any more so she was placed with her aunt. The aunt is unable to continue so they need to decide whether the child should be with a white family or Black family. I felt hurt in this discussion as I found that I had to defend and make a stand in being a Black person. It would have been nice if there had been another Black person to give some support. (student 2)

Teaching placements

If you were to ask any student, Black/ethnic minority or white, about their experience of their teaching placement, the majority would hesitate and then just say that they passed. The teaching placement is one of the students' worst nightmares and if you happen to be Black/ethnic minority you know that the placement is where you are most likely to fail. The teaching placement is the area that most students felt they would like to have more control over. Many students worried that they might be placed in schools in areas known for their high levels of racist activity. Given the relative powerlessness of all student teachers on teaching practice, it is perhaps not surprising that for Black students, this can be a time of extreme difficulty (Crozier and Menter, 1993). Iram Siraj-Blatchford's (1990, p.17) account of Black students' experiences of teacher education courses concludes that 'school practice provided the worst experience of racial discrimination for many Black students'. Some comments from the students in her survey indicate the quality of this experience:

> In an urban, mainly white school the older children, upper infants and juniors made racist comments such as 'Blacky' and 'Nigger'.

> I did a teaching practice in an urban multiracial school. I was placed in a class which is considered by both my tutors and teaching staff to be the worst they have ever seen. I was verbally and physically abused by the children. The only reason why I was placed there is because I was Black. They removed a white student yet disputed my pleas to leave, they would not let me. I am ignored by all of my staff. My class teacher treats me as if I am invisible, mainly because I disagree with the way the children are treated, i.e. constant suspensions rather than logical reasoning and a consistent approach.

In principle there have been some positive changes since the 1990 study, but Black students are still experiencing discrimination on teacher placement. The students interviewed in the HEFCE studies described some of their experiences:

> I was on my placement in Woking, I came out of school and I got stopped by the police, I was walking to the station, I'm in my suit, and I have with me my briefcase. I was stopped by the police, with questions like where are you going, where have you been. I didn't

expect that. I responded in an appropriate manner. I was then told that there had been a high increase in burglaries recently. (student 3)

I did not feel comfortable speaking to my tutors. The reason that I would not feel comfortable speaking to tutors previous to this is, as this is my final teaching practice, I don't think that they would have understood what I was speaking about really. Some things can happen to a Black person but to explain it is different from actually feeling it, because sometimes it is not a word that is spoken, it might be an action, or the way that you are treated, and then you get told that you are being paranoid, or you have a chip on your shoulder or surely you're imagining things. (student 4)

These students did not just have to face the 'race' issue on a daily basis but were made to feel that they should be hugely grateful when some support was actually offered to them.

My first and second year teaching placement, yes they did consider my needs. I discussed my domestic situation with them and they were very obliging, but I don't think that it something that they would do automatically. They made it perfectly clear that I should be eternally grateful that they were making an exception, I was going to a school very near to where I live, because I have children etc. They made it very clear that I was to be very grateful. (student 7)

The students felt strongly that they had been left to cope with racism on their own. None believed that the university had interceded on their behalf.

In the classroom

Many students find themselves isolated and might deal with their feelings by adopting certain behaviour. They may feel compelled to act out a stereotype, in an attempt to fit into the expected role. By so doing, they will internalise any racist vibes that surround them, and even deny their existence. The student is playing the game for the teacher, who holds the power to obstruct their success. Alternatively, students might choose to challenge teachers and other students over any issues or individuals regarding race. On reflection, one can see that such behaviour could also affect the student's well-being adversely. Worse still, the students may be expected to cope with harassment themselves and develop a strategy to deal with the problem, so shifting the responsibility from the teacher onto the learner. Students who take such responsibility will say that they tried their best and can at least hold their head high.

Conclusion

This chapter has let the students speak for themselves, so highlighting some of their recent experiences in initial teacher training. Many UK ITT institutions protest that they wish to recruit more students from Black/ethnic minority backgrounds and there is certainly a need for more Black teachers. The Black students in the various HEFCE studies, as is clear also in the other chapters, are representative of the wealth of talent and experience that such recruits bring into teaching.

It is not enough, however, merely to attract Black students onto courses. Universities and colleges need to review their practices to ensure that Black students are given fair treatment and equal rights to develop their skills and talents and to progress within the profession. Such treatment and such rights have to be embedded in the institutions' policy. Black/ethnic minority students are demanding the right to participate actively in their own education, and teacher educators must be aware of the ways in which racism can act as a barrier to effective and full participation by these students. Not only does each institution need to review its structures but well-intentioned individuals will have to acknowledge that intentions alone are no a guarantee of good practice; What counts is that outcomes are no longer discriminatory.

Racism may damage the life chances and educational opportunities of Black people, but individual experiences are diverse and complex and go beyond racism. So tutors need to be particularly careful not to assess their students according to racial criteria. Education for democracy and equal rights must be seen as essential in teacher education if all students are to develop into effective teachers, themselves capable of promoting equality and justice in schools. A full and explicit examination of issues of equity and social justice is vital but students need also to develop skills which enable them to be self-critical and to examine their own education; they need to be encouraged to explore their own values and to share responsibility with their tutors in identifying their needs and in decision-making. The next two sections of the book discuss what can be done. We have much to gain from these students, and their experience needs to be taken into account, if ITT institutions are seriously seeking to increase the numbers of Black/ethnic minority students entering teacher training and if those students are indeed to become teachers for the future.

Bibliography

Bansal, R. (1990) A Sikh by Night in *Times Educational Supplement:* 20 July.

Blair, M. and Maylor, U. (1993) 'Issues and concerns for Black Women Teachers in Training', in Siraj-Blatchford, I (ed) *'Race', Gender and the Education of Teachers.* Buckingham: Open University Press.

Boxill, B. (1991) 'Equality, discrimination and preferential treatment', in P. Singer (ed.) *A Companion to Ethics.* Oxford, Blackwell.

Brennan, J. and McGeevor, P. (1990) *Ethnic Minorities and the Graduate Labour Market.* London: CRE

Cohen, L. (1989) Ignorance, not Hostility: student teachers' perceptions of ethnic minorities in Britain, in Verma, G *Education for All: a landmark in pluralism.* Lewes: Famer

Commission for Racial Equality (1987) *Living in Terror.* London: CRE.

Commission for Racial Equality (1988a) *Ethnic Minority School Teachers.* London: CRE.

Commission for Racial Equality (1988b) *Learning in Terror:* London: CRE.

Connelly, C. (1993), Guidelines on Equal Opportunities for Ethnic Minority Students in Higher Education. Unpublished version for CRE.

Crozier, G. and Menter I. (1993), 'The Heart of the matter? student teachers' experiences in school', in Siraj-Blatchford, I (ed) *'Race', Gender And The Education Of Teachers.* Open University Press.

DES (1989b) Responses to Ethnic Diversity in Teacher Training, Circular 117/89. London: HMSO.

Haselgrove, S (1994) *The Student Experience,* Open University Press.

Henry, C., Drew J., Anwar, H., Campbell, G. and Benoit-Asselman, D. (1992) *The EVA Project Ethnics and Values Audit.* Preston, University of Central Lancashire.

Higher Education Funding Council for England (1993) *Assessors Handbook.* Bristol, HEFCE(E).

Higher Education Quality Council for England (1993) *Notes for the Guidance of Auditors.* Birmingham, HEQC (Division of Quality Audit).

Leicester, M. (1993) *Race for a Change in Continuing and Higher Education.* Open University Press.

Mac an Ghaill, M. (1988) *Young, Gifted and Black: student teacher relations in the schooling of Black youth.* Milton Keynes: Open University Press.

Mac an Ghaill, M. (1989) Coming of age in 1980s England: reconceptualizing Black students' schooling experience. *British Journal of Sociology of Education,* 10.

Mattai, P. Rudy (1995) *Redressing the Issues of Equity and Diversity in Academia: The Need for Systemic Institutional Changes.* State University of New York College at Buffalo.

Menter, I. (1987) 'Evaluating Teacher Education: some notes on an anti-racist programme for BEd students'. *Multicultural Teaching*, 5,3, 39-42

Milner, D. (1983) *Children and Race; ten years on.* Ward Lock, London.

Mirza, H. (1992) *Young, Female and Black.* London: Routledge.

Moody, C. (1995) *Strategies for Improving the Representation and Participation of Black Faculty, Students and Staff in Tertiary Education.* The University of Michigan

National Union of Students (1993) NUS *Student Charter.* London, NUS

Osler, A. (1994) *Education For Democracy and Equality: The experiences, values and attitudes of ethnic minority student teachers.* University of Birmingham

Rosen, V. (1993) Black students in higher education, in M. Thorpe, R. Edwards and A. Hanson (eds) *Culture and Process of Adults Learning.* London: Routledge in association with the Open University.

Siraj Blatchford, I. (1991) A Study of Black students' Perceptions of Racism in Initial Teacher Education. *British Educational Research Journal,* 17, 1, 35-50.

Siraj-Blatchford, I. (1993) *'Race', Gender and The Education of Teachers,* Open University Press

The Voice Newspaper. (July 4 1995. p.24)

Wright, C. (1986) Ethnographic study in *Education for Some* ed. by J. Eggleston *et.al.* Trentham Books

Wright, C. (1992) 'Early Education: Multiracial primary school classrooms', in Gill, D. Mayor, B and Blair, M (eds) *Racism and Education: structures and strategies.* Sage: London.

SECTION III
Supports and Strategies

Chapter 5

The Wise Teacher
The Role of Guidance Workers, Parents, Schools, Communities and ..... Admissions Tutors

Lisa Robinson

Admissions and Initial Teacher Training

I recently attended the annual CRAC conference, entitled 'Admissions to Higher Education' which took place this year (1995) at the University of Warwick. Throughout the three day event discussions focused around issues such as equality of opportunity, widening access and encouraging participation from groups which are under-represented in Higher Education. In addition to taking part in the general debate, I attended several optional workshops, including one which dealt with admissions issues on ITT courses. Three admissions tutors from chartered and new HEIs (Higher Education Institutions) presented their views on admissions policy, discussed the changes now taking place in ITT and answered questions from the delegates. I questioned them to establish the extent to which admissions tutors are in a position to influence the nature of the intake of undergraduates and indeed post-graduates (in the case of

PGCEs). I asked 'In the light of the fact there is a serious shortage of Black[1] students undertaking ITT and hence taking their place in the profession, are you doing anything to redress this imbalance?' The response of one tutor (accompanied by enthusiastic nodding from the others) was that admissions tutors could not activate 'Positive Action' in terms of screening applications.

I found their misinterpretation of the question disappointing and remain concerned about what was a narrow and, unfortunately, expected answer. The response typifies the stance of too many individuals in the sector and is based on an assumption that any practice relating to equality, widening access and making courses more representative of the communities they recruit from, could only find its voice in Positive Action[2] strategies — which remain unpopular. The admissions tutors' response clearly demonstrated that they did not consider it necessary to be involved in the nature of intake with regards to anything but numbers (satisfying quotas), and the qualifications held by individuals applying to them. Furthermore there was no concept of being able to influence the nature of each cohort of students, or indeed having any responsibility to influence who becomes a teacher for the future.

Workers from the HEFCE projects have taken issue with this concern (the roles and responsibilities of admissions tutors) in their joint meetings over the last year. I hope the future role of admissions tutors will develop an emphasis on proactive involvement in the marketing of courses and the recruitment, guidance and fostering of potential applicants. For the present, it is apparent that admissions tutors, generally, represent a commonly held belief that it is the responsibility of those involved in guidance *per se* to ensure that well suited Black students are making applications — another stock expression we have come to expect from many admissions tutors is that 'Black students simply don't apply'. People involved in guidance retain a key role in widening participation for Black students.

Guidance Practice

A chapter about guidance and nurturing inevitably demands some discussion about what constitutes guidance and who gives it. The Black community, similarly to other communities, uses both the informal and formal structures available to them. Any map of a 'guidance community' will include careers services, training institutions, TECs, community organisations and so forth. Individuals also go to friends, other professionals and most importantly their parents, for advice and information about their future pathways.

The nature of guidance given by individuals is partly dependent upon whether the provider is part of the formal or informal guidance community. Formal guidance practice is based on operational principles which vary from institution to institution. Nottingham Trent University has recently developed the Certificate in Careers Guidance. Below I have listed the operational principles which they highlight.

Careers Guidance Operational Principles

The Client is the primary decision maker

The Adviser is obliged to manage the process of the interview to ensure that it delivers appropriate outcomes for the client

The Institution is obliged to provide an environment and the resources necessary to deliver Careers Guidance.

Ground rules will be established and maintained, through a process of negotiation, to ensure that:

— *Adviser and client can be honest with each other. Adviser and client are actively engaged in the interview*

— *Adviser and client both understand what is taking place throughout the interview*

— *Shared information is used only for agreed purposes*

— *Adviser and client each take responsibility for adhering to any contractual agreements into which they enter with one another.*

Few would disagree with the qualities expected in the list. However, such operational principles do not take account of the question of objectivity and the ability to respond to the diverse needs of the students with which guidance practitioners work. These issues become pertinent when considering the needs of Black clients. In terms of remaining objective, I suggest that the preconceptions, possible ignorance and racism of the adviser/guidance worker, too often work to influence 'good' guidance practice. Assessment is essential to guidance practice: subjectivity will inevitably creep in. Audrey Osler (1994) in her paper 'Education For

Democracy and Equality — The Experiences Values and Attitudes of Ethnic Minority Student Teachers', states that as well as schools having poor expectations of them, few students benefited from formal careers advice. As part of the HEFCE Project I worked on with Wolverhampton University, I too carried out research into the experiences of Black students (including mature students) on ITT courses. Here are some of their comments with regards to careers/education guidance which they received:

> When I left college I wanted to go into teaching. The tutor put me off.

> I wanted to do it (teaching) when I was at school... but was advised by careers for typing or nursing. In those days Black people weren't supposed to do anything like that (teaching).

> Teaching is something I've wanted to do for a long time. My interview with the careers officer put me off. They suggested nursery nursing.

> I was told not to do A levels. The careers teacher advised me to do a YTS. I brought myself here...no one believed in me.

> Careers advice centres should do more to promote teaching..from a Black point of view. I had no encouragement from the careers office at school.

Ilham Abou Rahme (1995) discusses the research she carried out with HE students at four different universities in the UK. She asked about guidance received at various stages in their education (11-16, 16-18,18-21 and 21+). She concludes:

> There is very low correlation between age of students interviewed and Careers Officers' understanding of their needs. This implies that over time there has been an insignificant improvement in the Careers Officers' understanding of the needs of students of ethnic origin.

Rahme points out that students at 18 are more likely to challenge the advice they receive — a more in-depth study might suggest that younger people are far more vulnerable to having their confidence and motivation undermined by formal guidance processes.

Careers *advice* is often given in the place of *guidance* — that is, impartial and objective guidance. The prejudices/preconceptions of careers advisers all to often act as a barrier to the aspirations of Black 'clients'. I do not feel that this is recognised in the operational principles underlying the practice undertaken. All too often practitioners themselves do not appreciate that working with Black clients actually demands, in many cases, a difference in approach.

When writing this chapter, I had a long discussion with a friend and colleague, Millie Weir, an education and careers adviser at Coventry University and the chair of the National Black Careers Advisers Group (NBCAG). We talked about how guidance should reflect a Black client's needs and she talked about her philosophy of the guidance worker being like a 'wise teacher'. From a teacher who is wise we would have certain minimum expectations. As well as being well informed, able to relate to and communicate with individuals' needs (on the basis of their sex, race, nationality etc), being able to educate or make wise their students, the wise teacher should also expect the best from their students. It is not enough to be objective; the wise teacher encourages the student to want the best for themselves and to aim high. As Nasim Ali, Juliet Cook and Ann Ryan (1994) point out: 'One of the most important areas where misjudgements and the undervaluing of potential are likely to take place is in the assessment of young (Black) people's abilities and aspirations'. Their observation that it is not enough to have more Black workers providing the advice is acute for two reasons. Firstly, the Service itself is not encouraged to think about what it can do by way of change and secondly:

> they (Black workers) are frequently expected to undertake most or all of the specialist work with Black young people. They are often expected to be able to relate as experts to all Black clients, even though they may be unfamiliar with the language and culture of many of the ethnic groups they serve (ibid).

The ability to relate to and communicate with all clients and the skill to react to cultural, racial and linguist difference without sacrificing high expectation is an essential quality in the wise teacher/guidance worker. Advisers, whether Black or white, should strive to 'get wise' to the needs of all their clients — it is interesting to note that over half of the white careers advisers interviewed in the research felt unable, or were unsure as to their ability to help young Black people. Seventy five percent of the students interviewed in Rhame's sample (ibid) showed that Careers Officers did not understand the needs and aspirations of ethnic minority students at the age of 16.

The evidence suggests that race education and awareness training should be sought by those working in guidance. It is imperative that Service managers make adequate provision in staff development programmes for staff to address issues of race which affect their practice. Guidance practitioners cannot be said to be truly qualified in terms of working with Black clients until they have received adequate training. Resources need to be developed to support training and staff development. The BBC in conjunction with the Institute of Careers Guidance have recently released a videopack: *MOSAIC, Fair Guidance.* Complete with trainers' notes, it explores issues around guidance with minority communities. *Educational Guidance with Black Communities — a checklist for good practice* has been on the market for some time. We need more extensive resources to be developed to support training and staff development. In addition, training resources which do not specifically address race should in future include a race perspective where appropriate.

Nurturing

In terms of guidance practice, I have, so far, concentrated on the formal structures of guidance and on guidance professionals. The part which community organisations, schools and parents have to play in guidance is crucial to the careers education of Black children — they, especially, have a role in nurturing the aspirations of students, since they, unlike guidance workers, spend much more time with the young people themselves. Students involved in the research at Wolverhampton University identified teachers and family members as the people who nurtured their interest and preparation for entry into ITT. In recognition of this, a key objective of the Wolverhampton project was to carry out work with schools, parents and community groups, setting up workshops and disseminating information into the wider community which, for the use of parents whose first language is not English, was available in the main Asian languages used by people in that region.

The potential of schools to increase the participation of Black students onto ITT courses is self-evident. Who better to provide guidance with regards to the teaching profession than teachers themselves? Unfortunately, due to the lack of training of teachers involved in giving careers/education guidance and factors of racism, mainstream schools do not generally have a good reputation for inspiring our Black youngsters.

As for Guidance Workers, the curriculum used to train teachers does not address race and cultural difference adequately and Black students are often placed at a disadvantage.

In any case, young people are more likely to look to parents rather than teachers for careers ideas. In 1992 NFER carried out research for the National Commission on Education which investigated the experiences and attitudes of 11 and 13 year old students. They asked, amongst other things, 'to whom do younger students talk about their career plans?' Approximately 90% of 13 year olds said they sometimes or often talked to their parents. About 50% said they never talked to their teachers. The two researchers who undertook the work reported their findings at the BP/UCAS Conference 1995 Promoting Higher Education to Younger Age Groups. The conference report summed up the response to this research well:

> This emphasises the importance of ensuring that parents have information about the range of jobs open to their children and the qualifications needed for different careers. There may also be a message here for schools: perhaps schools should make greater efforts to involve younger students in discussions about career options, qualifications and further/higher education.

Recommendations

If schools and parents are to equip themselves with adequate resources (both human and material) to carry out guidance practice, they will need to go to the 'experts'. This brings the onus back on careers/education guidance workers to develop, perfect and effect appropriate guidance practice. Partnerships between schools, parents and external guidance practitioners need to be discussed, developed and solidified. Parents' evenings are an example of a forum within which such a partnership could be established. ACE (Aiming for a College Education) has issued useful guidelines around structuring parents' evenings to meet the needs of Black and ethnic minority pupils.

Guidance practice needs to be filtered into the curriculum of educational institutions, making that curriculum vocationally relevant — including HEIs where undergraduates might consider PGCEs. Vocationally relevant curricula need to be in place at all ability levels and, where classes are streamed, the options available should not be limited to perceived ability but should, instead, encourage self-development and meet and nurture high aspirations.

Higher Education personnel working in the field of community and school liaison need to target organisations with high proportions of ethnic minority pupils. Mentoring and tutoring schemes have proved their worth in relation to guidance and nurturing of career aspirations of young Black people.[3]

Training courses that are for guidance practitioners and teachers need to include a race perspective, and resources need to be developed in order to enhance formal training and self-development.

In conclusion, I return to the admissions tutor in HE who gatekeeps the intake of students to the institution's courses. The ongoing changes in ITT, the developments concerning the structuring of courses, and the knowledge of what admissions tutors are looking for are crucial to candidates who need to be well informed. Admissions tutors, and all staff involved in the recruitment strategies of HEIs, need to look beyond positive action as a formal policy and towards *positive action* in their admissions practice, to ensure that the guidance imparted to our future teachers enables them to get over the major hurdle of the selection process.

Notes

1.   'Black' is used here to denote all people from 'visible' ethnic minority groups.
2.   The issue of Positive Action, in relation to admissions policy is addressed in chapter ... of this publication.
3.   For example, the Wolverhampton project successfully trained Black students to act as role models to Black pupils in schools and carry out sessions about teacher training and HE more generally to non-segregated classes across year and ability groups.

References

Nasim Ali, Juliet Cook, Ann Ryan, 'Processing Black Clients: A Careers Service perspective', in *Black Youth Futures,* 1994

BBC and The Institute of Careers Guidance *MOSAIC Project, Fair Guidance,* 1993

Stella Dadzie, *Educational Guidance with Black Communities — A checklist for good practice*, NIACE REPLAN, 1990

Audrey Osler, Education for Democracy and Equality — The Experiences, Values and Attitudes of Ethnic Minority Student Teachers (Conference paper) 1994

Ilham Abou Rahme, 'How Do You Rate in the 'Impartial Guidance' Stakes?' *Careers Guidance Today* Vol 3 (1) Spring 1995.

Chapter 6

The Black Goddess:
a perspective on Mentoring

Victoria Showunmi

Background to the projects

How well students do in Higher Education depends not only on their abilities but also on the support they receive. It has been known since the inception of access courses over a decade ago that non-standard entry students and ethnic minority students are the two (not necessarily separate) groups that find HE institutions, for one reason or another, less welcoming than do white anglophone young people from grammar streams or public schools.

Mentoring, then, finds its natural candidates among Black/ethnic minority and access students. When mentoring or other support is effective, these students do well. Kingston University brought mentoring into the HEFCE project, one of the seventeen, for which it bid successfully.

Its initial plan was to devise and implement strategies over one year to increase the number of ethnic minority students entering teacher training at Kingston University, and to determine any special requirements for their support while they studied and possibly after graduation. The project focused on African, Caribbean, Asian and Chinese trainee teachers currently at the University, with a view to examining the reasons why they chose teaching as a career, the academic career path they took, and the type of support that they required during their training.

Parallel to the academic research side of this study, it was decided that a Mentorship scheme should be established. This would allow mentees such as school pupils, college and university students who were considering teaching as career, the opportunity to be mentored by a new graduate teacher, or to shadow a practising teacher of the same ethnic background. As well as determining the special requirements of the proposed support in teacher training, it was decided that the academic side of this project should conduct an extensive investigation of existing and recently graduated trainee teachers from an urban university in the UK.

Project Two

A project involving three universities based in rural areas in the UK obtained funding as part of the Flexibility in Teaching and Learning Scheme. According to the 1991 census, there are 63,000 Black/ethnic minority people in this rural area in the North of England, and consultation with representatives of communities in both the outer and inner region confirms that there is considerable concern both about their representation in the professions and about the experience of Black/ethnic minority students in Higher Education. A recent analysis of UCCA data indicates marked Black/ethnic differences in rates of admission to university. The project aims to inform members of Black/ethnic minority communities about opportunities in Higher Education and about encouraging an ethos in universities which will encourage and support Black/ethnic minority students.

The project has highlighted four main factors that will need to be considered throughout its life span: institutional development, community participation, mentoring and liaison with existing HEFCE projects. The four factors will interconnect with other issues such as: recruitment/ selection, the ethos, marketing, career guidance, fair interviewing, dealing with harassment, and academic supervision and assessment. As an education consultant, I was asked to develop a mentor scheme for Black/ethnic minority students who are already on a course of study at the universities and for potential applicants considering a place at one of the three. Due to the time span, the mentor scheme would be for Teacher Education only.

The Origins of Mentoring

The use of the word *mentor* is becoming more prevalent to the point of being a 'buzz-word'. However, the concept of mentoring is not just another Americanism. It has a very long history. The word mentor comes from Greek mythology; it appears in Homer's *Odyssey*, circa 800 BC. Mentor, Athena the goddess of wisdom in a human guise, was the companion of Odysseus, King of Ithaca. His duty was to raise the King's son to be fit for the crown. Mentor was required to be father figure, advisor, encourager and educator.

Mentoring has developed as a deliberate pairing of a more skilled or experienced person with one less skilled or experienced, with the agreed goal of having the lesser skilled person grow and develop specific competencies. Various programmes exist, as described by Kram and Isabella (1985). They suggest that peers can provide career and psychosocial functions similar to those found in hierarchical mentoring alliances. The pairing of peers for mutual support may be in effect mentoring but I would not use the term to describe such an arrangement. Similarly, a systematic approach to organisational change sometimes called organisational development, for implementing a mentoring process, has been described by others (Beer, 1980; Kram and Isabella, 1985). Merely changing the structure of the organisation will not result in an effective mentoring programme. The research that I have undertaken in relation to mentoring has led me to believe that mentor schemes fall into those which emphasise the professional development of the mentee and those concerned with both their professional and their personal development. Together, they provide the basis of at least four different approaches to mentoring:

One: For professional gain, mainly used in the private sector for employee personal and career development of employees.

Two: Government initiative for teacher training. Due to the push towards school-based teacher training, mentors are provided in all school placements. The mentors in turn gain career development and enhancement for management training.

Three: Support aimed at young Black/ethnic minority students in Further and Higher Education, to provide a support mechanism while they pursue their education.

Four: School-based mentor schemes aimed at school pupils. The mentor is a professional person/volunteer, able to share experience and knowledge with young people.

For a Mentor scheme to be successful, it needs to be based on:

- a design that meets the perceived needs of the organisation
- a set of criteria and a process for the selection of the mentors
- strategies for matching mentors and mentees
- a negotiated agreement between mentor and mentee
- formative evaluation so that adjustments can be made to the programme as needed
- summative evaluation to determine outcomes for the organisation, mentors and mentees
- a sound training scheme for both mentors and mentees.

In the educational world, mentoring has recently achieved notoriety because of the way it has been developed within teacher education. Kenneth Clarke, the former Minster for Education, suggested that student teachers should receive most of their training on the job from 'mentors' — experienced teachers with special responsibility for trainee teachers (quoted in Burton and Wiener 1993). In his speech to the North of England Education Conference in January 1992, Clarke said: 'I find the concept of the 'mentors,' teachers with a particular responsibility for a student or groups of students, an attractive one' (para.2.5).

Mentoring has been used in the formal sense in industry and commerce and, more informally, in most parts of the public and private sectors. Burton and Wiener (1993) found, when they analysed their information, that the notion of mentoring is neither simple nor uniform. The interviewees who formed part of their research mentioned mentoring with respect either to actual mentors or to particular people who had been significant to career development. As one of their interviewees said: 'The Head of Department was a Mentor to me. He constantly offered debriefing on my lessons and classroom skills. If one is open to it, I find mentoring systems very effective'.

The Windsor Fellowship, concerned with fostering Black achievement, defines mentoring as: 'the means by which experienced and successful individuals take a younger person under his/her wing, offering advice, support and encouragement. Burton and Wiener (1993) looked at mentoring from the angle of teachers employed in the system. The sample of students interviewed for the Kingston research confirmed that for Black trainee teachers, having a mentor provided support in a professional and learning environment, in relation to the sociological indicators of race and gender.

Ian Menter (1989) suggests that race and gender are both significant factors in the reproduction of inequality in and throughout education, so are important issues in their own right, that they are indeed contemporary educational issues. The extent of response to these issues in educational sites can be an indicator of the effectiveness of the institution or school in delivering the curriculum. Some versions of antiracism and anti-sexism are certaining espoused by many teacher educators and were explicitly required within Initial Teacher Training courses by the former Council for the Accreditation of Teacher Education. Even so Menter questions the practical consequences and the extent to which such requirements influenced the courses as delivered. And the Teacher Training Agency does not stipulate that there be assessed units on race or gender issues. So support has to be at an individual level.

Aims of the Black/ethnic minority Mentor Scheme

The aim of the mentor project is to provide support and guidance for Black/ethnic minority students upon entering higher education institutions. One hopes that the support of mentors will enable the mentees to stay on within the education system and to establish networks after they have graduated.

The objectives of a mentoring scheme in HE as developed in Kingston University were:

- to enable Higher Education institutions to raise their profile in schools by meeting local community needs
- to provide opportunities for Black/ethnic minority students in Higher Education

- to enable students and professionals to share experiences and develop strategies to overcome barriers within the education system
- to encourage pupils in schools to develop a more positive view of Higher Education through contact with students / professionals as role models
- to contribute to the personal development of students in both Higher Education and schools, through shared communication and co-operation, and to encourage the growth of transferable skills
- to provide a platform for both students and professionals to network
- to develop management skills required for progression
- to give support and guidance to potential and existing students
- to bring together Higher Education, Further Education, schools and professional bodies.

How the Mentor scheme works

The scheme described was a unique process whereby enthusiastic and motivated professionals were linked with African, African-Caribbean, Asian and Chinese students in school, Further Education or Higher Education. Each mentee was matched with a mentor who shared the same career aims. Through careful matching, the mentees gained valuable knowledge and experience from their professional mentors.

The programmes developed in relation to the Black/ethnic minority community are significant models. In Programme A the mentees are mentored by Black/ethnic minority professionals. In Programme B the mentors are white and the students are Black/ethnic minority. Each scheme involves the notion of peer support and work-place shadowing. However, both the mentor and mentee must be able to allocate at least two to three hours per month to the programme over the six months period. The scheme only works if the mentor and mentee both wish it to. In other words you can only gain as much as you put into the 'mentor relationship'.

The Benefits of Mentoring

The teachers involved in the Kingston mentor scheme supported the idea for two main reasons. Firstly, because it enabled African, African-Caribbean, Asian and Chinese students to gain support and guidance from qualified teachers who reflected their own culture. Secondly, the scheme created the opportunity for some of the students to work in a multicultural environment, which some of the trainee teachers had not yet experienced whilst on teaching placements. One African origin primary school teacher said:

> As ethnic minority teachers we should see ourselves as role models to ethnic minority children in our schools and also to the society at large.

The pilot mentor scheme has, moreover, increased the students' confidence about choosing teaching as a career. The students felt that the mentor project should continue and become an integral part of the course. Such a scheme would enable students to have support while at university, from either fellow students or qualified teachers. One African-Caribbean student remarked: 'It would definitely help those coming in September'.

Another said:

> I think it is going to be useful; at least our voice is being heard at last. We are on this course and nobody takes the time to think whether we have encountered any racism or not, no one has even bothered to ask us what it has been like for us as Black students.

It seems that the aim of education for a multicultural society permeating courses across the curriculum (ARTEN 1988) has generally not been achieved and certainly not in some institutions. There is considerable evidence that ITT courses have been reactive and have failed to actively promote anti-racism. Educationalists have argued for courses in a multicultural society to be concerned with providing understandings of race, equality and power structures as well as cultural factors (Milner, 1983; Troyna, 1987).

Overall, the Kingston Mentor Scheme has been excellent in raising the profile of ethnic minority students within the university. The mentor programme acts as a positive form of networking for African, African-Caribbean and Asian students. It enables students to come together and, moreover, to establish that their problems are not unique to them alone. Such knowledge gives students power and builds upon developing their confidence. The evidence will be apparent in the amount of funding to be made available for staff development and for equal opportunities implementation throughout the university.

For all the HEFCE projects, it is hoped that action will be taken to ensure that the initiatives will not merely become another marketing tool to encourage African, African-Caribbean and Asian students into Higher Education without providing the support they need to enable them to pass their chosen course. A Code of Practice is needed for equal opportunities, for both the schools and the university to adhere to while students are out on placement. A Code will equip the university with a clear statement to the schools when they send students out on placement and any school that is involved with the placements will have prior knowledge of the Code of Practice.

Factors for success

An important factor in the development of Mentor Schemes is the notion of clear aims and objectives for both the mentors and mentees. As a consultant/researcher, I would fully endorse the mentor scheme as a possible support mechanism for students of African, African-Caribbean, Asian and Chinese origin whilst at university and during their probation in schools. Mentees and mentors needed more time than the one year project allowed, to establish a relationship before embarking as a team. This problem aside, mentors and mentees both felt that it was an excellent idea and needed to be continued.

Some students said that the support and guidance they had been given by their mentors really helped them to get through the year. In the words of one:

> I know I would have been really glad to have had this type of thing, especially the mentor scheme. When I first started this course, and when I was going through all the wrangle, just from one comment in the second year, it seems that ever since that time so many of them are against me.

Another student supported the mentor scheme thus:

> I think this entire scheme is a really good idea. I was hoping also not just to be a mentor or a mentee but I wouldn't have minded the idea of getting into some school, with the age groups of 11-13 where they are just beginning to look at what they are going to do for GCSEs.

Students benefited by networking with other students and exchanging practical methods for dealing with problems they faced. The feedback from the students was positive and the main feelings were that the project should become a central part of the next academic year. This would encourage new students joining the university and interested sixth formers who would like a 'taster' into what teaching is all about.

The Mentor chain process

All the Black/ethnic minority students based in the faculty of education were given the opportunity to take part in the pilot mentor scheme at the university. Twenty five students took part in the scheme initially. Six were sixth formers and the others were trainee teachers from the university. I would like to take you through the practical side of this mentor process.

The chain process of mentoring is an unique model. The chain starts with school, links into further education and then continues straight through to the university sector. The student mentee is able to have a choice of mentors with different ranges of experience.

The six form mentee is mentored by either a trainee teacher from the university or a professional teacher from school, further education or university. The trainee teacher mentee is mentored by either trainee teachers in a higher year or a professional teacher. Both mentees are able to chose if they would like another student or a professional teacher as their mentor. Some mentors had the opportunity to mentor both a six form student and a trainee teacher. This chain process of mentoring really enables the mentees and mentors involved to develop a relationship which will support and guide mentees while they complete their studies.

How to get the process from the drawing board into reality

Stage one: The university

An introduction meeting was arranged for interested trainee teachers from the university and agencies who could suggest Black/ethnic minority teachers in the neighbouring borough. Both the trainee teachers and the professionals were able to obtain an in-depth account of the project aims and objectives of the mentor scheme. At the meeting the mentors were allocated a small discussion area, with the idea that the interested mentees would spend five minutes with each mentor just talking in general. I felt that this kind of networking enabled both parties to get a feel of what the mentoring process is all about.

Stage two: the school

Another introductory meeting was arranged, this time for teachers and pupils in the Ealing area. With the help from the inspector I was able to link up with two schools with sixth forms. Again the meeting allowed everyone time to understand the project and the aims of the mentor scheme. The student mentees were inspired to see that there were Black/ethnic minority professionals who are successful and have made it in the system. After the general talk the interested mentors and mentees split into two groups and questions were asked and answered. It was the first time that the students were able to network, and to acknowledge that teachers are much like them and face the same fears and barriers in their everyday life. It was a very positive meeting, with both mentors and mentees eager to sign up for the project.

Stage three: the networking process

I decided that for both the mentors and the mentees to benefit from the process and feel at ease, only Black/ethnic minority people should attend this crucial meeting. It was essential to get this initial meeting right so that the whole process could develop into positive mentoring relationships. The project manager was there at the start and then, as arranged, she was asked to leave so that each interested person could gain some confidence in the scheme. One needs to acknowledge at every stage that Black people need to feel at ease before they talk. Mentor and mentee must feel comfortable with one another before making a contract. The mentee must feel in control of the interactions. It is far easier and quicker — and the customary practice — for the institution to pair up mentees with their mentors but far more effective if mentees can select their own mentors. In this case, the mentors were placed in small buzz groups around the room. The mentees were then asked to spend ten minutes with each of the mentors to have a general discussion in the area of career choice, barriers and success. Each mentor was able to speak to a maximum five mentees at one time. All the mentees were provided with a sheet of paper so they could note who they would like as a mentor. The student mentee could be mentored by either a student or a professional teacher or both. Mentors were only allowed to mentor two students throughout the project.

Stage four: maintaining contact

The mentors and mentees were encouraged to exchange telephone numbers and addresses so that they could contact each other. They were asked to make contact within a fortnight, to arrange their first meeting. For the mentor and mentee to establish a partnership they to meet at least once every three weeks. But for these meetings to be a success clear outlines are needed to establish the reasons for each meeting. And there has to be someone at the head of the project who is aware of all the issues and can support all the people concerned. The mentors and mentees were able to contact me at any time during work or at home. To maintain good contact with all the mentors and mentees one needs to have motivation, bags of energy and a good sense of direction! Every six weeks the mentors and mentees were encouraged to attend a meeting so we could establish how the process went.

Stage five: evaluation

Each mentor and mentee was expected to produce a report at the end of the project. The reports were the only way for a written account of the process to be documented so that the good practice could be developed and disseminated. The teachers were able to use their mentor experience towards credits on a teacher management course. The student mentors could benefit by listing their achievement in their profile. More informally, a meeting of all those involved in the scheme — and including the Vice Chancellor of the university — allowed a general discussion of the strengths and weaknesses of the scheme.

Case study

Student

The student describes herself as an African-Caribbean woman who lives at home with her mother. She is a mature student who returned to study after deciding to fulfil her long term ambition to become a teacher. The specialist subject that she has chosen is English and Drama. The education system had lowered her expectations of herself so it took time to build up her confidence to step back onto the ladder. One of the main factors holding her back is racism. In Higher Education this came from her student placement and the university and was either very subtle and hence difficult to explain or, more recently, took the form of verbal abuse. Whilst on teacher placement there was an atmosphere which made her feel that the teachers were antagonistic towards her. What kept her going is her strong identification with her culture and the support and understanding she received from friends and family. However, the support from the university was less positive. She comments:

> I feel that especially on this course, that racism is not dealt with within the staff and the student body. Even if you felt that you had been racially harassed, I really don't feel that there is anybody I could go to and say look, this is what happened, and what are you going to do about it.

The mentor scheme came at an appropriate time, providing support and guidance from an African teacher who taught in the primary sector but had extensive experience in the secondary sector. The mentor she was allocated provided her with a friend and, above all, a Black woman who understands the system.

Whilst on placement she felt that she, personally, had become the school's Black experience. One of the elements which sticks are the stereotypes held by the pupils in her placement school. The attitude of the teachers forbade any discussion in relation to racism.

One mentee's account of mentoring

by Iris Tapper

When I heard about the mentor scheme I had mixed feelings, which included gladness, suspicion and relief. I say relief because after being in Kingston university for some time prior to this scheme I was glad to know that perhaps I'd get some support as a Black student. The university did have some lecturers who offered some support but nothing can beat someone who's actually walked a mile in your shoes. It's as the saying goes, 'those who feels it knows it', and having a Black person as a mentor would mean that they would know it. The mentor that I had was someone who my spirit took to immediately. The advice that she gave me was invaluable as well as the support. As well as this she is a really beautiful

Diary of a mentor: by Elizabeth Ibisiki Kalio

First mentee: Iris Tapper
Second mentee: Samantha Spence (herself mentored by Iris Tapper)

Iris Tapper

After Iris's name was officially given to me as my mentee, I rang her up, then sent a letter arranging a meeting. We met at a cafe and, over coffee, we discussed what the project is all about and what is expected of us. We then chatted about growing up in Britain as someone from an ethnic minority group. We had a long and useful talk about being a teacher or a trainee teacher. We came to some conclusions:

- *we as ethnic minority teachers should see ourselves as role models to ethnic minority children in our schools and also to society at large.*
- *we should offer counselling to children with apparent behavioural problems by liaising with the parents — a factor we consider to be very important in the teaching and learning process.*
- *since modern teaching places the child at the centre of all learning activities we should try and discourage the armchair psychologists among our colleagues who tend to marginalise children from ethnic minority backgrounds (Iris and I share similar experiences on this issue).*

Even though this meeting was of an introductory and social nature we were both happy to note that we have a lot in common and share similar aspirations.

Second meeting. I invited Iris to an African cultural evening on 11th June, to promote African cultural awareness to children and youths who were born in Britain and to raise money for projects in the Third World. Iris came with her sister and we had an enjoyable evening. As the president of the union, I told Iris that I intend to develop some of the activities of the evening into a resource pack for schools to use.

Third meeting. School visit — observation. On the 14th June, Iris came to my school to observe me teach. She spent half of the day in my class and participated fully in the activities I set out for the day. She was quite pleased with the disciplined nature of my five year olds. We agreed that if a teacher has high expectations of children they will achieve well. After the visit I took Iris to my house to meet my family.

Iris has promised to come for a whole day observation before the summer term ends.

Samantha Spence

I arranged to meet Samantha, again at a cafe. We introduced ourselves and discussed the project and why we are participating in it. Sam was very much aware of the problems of growing up in an international community and becoming a teacher. We discussed the students union set-up at the university and agreed that even though students' welfare is what the student union is all about, it will be a good idea to set up an ethnic minority unit to discuss problems specifically affecting ethnic minority students. Sam has a project in mind and is working on it.

Probationary year. Sam and I discussed the problems of what new teachers from Black/ethnic minority backgrounds might have to face on their first assignment. For example Sam was told in some of her teaching practice that children will not like her dreadlocks. Some Heads may not know how to tackle these problems. Should such a thing recur, what steps is the new teacher going to take?

I have tried to arrange for Sam to come over to my school to observe me teach but workload has prevented her from doing so. She hopes to come over before the school term ends.

On Reflection. I have thoroughly enjoyed this project and hope to continue. The reasons for this are compelling:

- *it has enabled me to make contact with people who share the same aspirations as I do.*

- *it is quite satisfying to meet these new teachers-to-be and share ideas on how to make the teaching and learning process meaningful.*

- *Iris and I are now family friends and hope to go on holiday together to Africa so that she will be able to appreciate her roots.*

More importantly for the scheme's future:

Iris and Sam are quite happy to be teachers and hoped to remain in the profession.

Judging from their enthusiasm, Iris and Sam will do well as Black teachers and be role models to the children they teach.

---

person in heart and physic. I'm glad that I had the opportunity to be part of the scheme and be mentored.

I was also assigned to be a mentor to someone else and I did find it difficult with the demands of my own life. The time that I was able to make contact was a real enjoyment and good for my self-esteem, as it surprised me that anyone would want advice from me. I must say that I think it's an excellent idea to have such a scheme, especially in a university that is so predominantly white, both students and lecturers. Im glad that Vicky had the insight to start such a scheme and I hope and pray that it will not be just an experiment but something that can continue.

Future plans

If time had permitted, the chain process would have continued beyond the mentees' study life at university into their first post after graduation. This would have allowed the mentees to be mentored throughout their first year of teaching. However, trying to conduct formal research and set up a mentor scheme was in fact rather problematic and there need to be at least two full time researchers to ensure that the aim and clear goals are meet by both the HEI mentors and mentees. I would also recommend that there is a need for a clear structure of mentoring to be embedded in the university as whole and not in fragments with no clear management direction. Where a mentor scheme is actually targeting race and racism, any HEI that adopts a mentor scheme should be sensitive to the wishes of the mentees about their choice of mentors and should put management of the scheme wholly into the hands of a Black/ethnic minority project leader. If the scheme described proved nothing else, it did prove that this was the major reason that it worked so well.

The Future of Mentoring

For a mentor scheme targeted specificially at Black and ethnic minority students to succeed, the university has to place its trust with the Black manager. Expecting a Black manager to make all decisions just as a white manager might is an unacceptable form of tokenism: the issue is one of perspective, not merely of visibility. That said, mentoring can be used as a positive approach to support Black/ethnic minority students in an educational context. One needs to remember that the work-place ethos of educational institutions is important not only for those who are employed there but also for those who attend as learners. With suitable guidance and support from appropriate mentors, learners of African, African-Caribbean, Asian and Chinese origin will more readily go into Higher Education. However, for mentoring to fulfil all requirements, there needs to be the appropriate resources and institutional support to allow the mentees to progress. And all parties in the institution need to recognise the benefits in the development of a Mentor Scheme and support it.

Bibliography

Arora, Ranjit, (1992), *Teacher Education and Ethnic Minorities*. Race Relations Research Unit, Bradford.

Bedfordshire Study (1992), 'Asian Young People, Career Intentions and Teaching, final draft 12th June, Bedfordshire County Council.

Blair, Maud and Maylor, Uvanney (1993) 'Issues and Concerns for Black Women Teachers in Training', in Siraj-Blatchford, Iram,(ed.) *'Race', Gender and the Education of Teachers*. Open University Press, Milton Keynes.

Brennan, John and McGregor, Philip (1990) *Ethnic Minorities and The Graduate Labour Market*, Council for National Academic Awards.

Burton, Leone and Weiner, Gaby (1993) 'From rhetoric to reality: strategies for developing a social justice approach to educational decision-making, in Siraj-Blatchford, *op. cit.*

Clay, John and George Rosalyn (1993), 'Moving Beyond Permeation: Courses in Teacher Education', in Siraj-Blatchford, *op. cit.*

Clay, John, Gadhla Sangita and Wilkins Chris, Racism and Institutional Inertia: A 3D perspective of Initial Teacher Education (disillusionment, disaffection and despair), *Multicultural Teaching* Vol 9 No 3.

Commission For Racial Equality (1988) *Learning In Terror: a survey of racial harassment in schools and colleges.* CRE, London.

Commission For Racial Equality (1993), *Code of Practice: For the Elimination of Racial Discrimination and The Promotion of Equality of Opportunity In Employment.* Interlink Longraph Limited.

Commission For Racial Equality (1993) *Code Of Practice: For The Elimination Of Racial Discrimination* In Education. CRE

Connelly, Clara, (1993) Guidelines on Equal Opportunities for Ethnic Minority Students In Higher Education, (unpublished version for CRE).

Crozier, Gill and Menter Ian, (1993) 'The Heart of the Matter', Student Teachers' Experiences in School' in Siraj-Blatchford, *op. cit.*

Gibson, Ashton and Barrow, Jocelyn (1986) *The Unequal, Struggle.* Centre For Caribbean Studies, Caribbean House.

Kram, K.E. and Isabella, L. (1985) 'Mentoring alterations: the role of peer relationships in career development, *Academy of Management Journal*, 28(1), pp.166.

Menter Ian, (1989) Teaching Practice Stasis: racism, sexism and school experience in Initial Teacher Education, *British Journal of Sociology of Education*, Vol.10.No.4.

Siraj-Blatchford, Iram. (1993) *'Race', Gender and The Education Of Teachers.* Open University Press, Milton Keynes.

Taylor Paul, (1992) *Higher Education Quarterly.* (Autumn)

Troyna, Barry, (1993) *Racism and Education research perspectives.* Open University Press, Milton Keynes.

University of London Institute of Education (1988) *'Opportunity For All'*, University Of London.

Wright, Nigel (1989) *Assessing Radical Education: a critical review of the radical movements in English Schooling 1960-1980.*

Chapter 7

Encouraging Access: Language Across the ITT Curriculum

Eleftheria Maria Neophytou, Sui-Mee Michelle Chan and Patricia East

Introduction

The School of Teaching Studies at the University of North London has been engaged in the professional preparation of teachers for inner city schools since 1967 and it has built up a reputation for high academic and vocational standards. The School has a successful graduate employment record, with 90% of students going on to teach in schools in the London area. The School is committed to encouraging access to initial teacher training (ITT) from all sections of the local community. It has a long tradition of attracting applicants from ethnic community groups which are under-represented in the teaching profession.

Recruitment from ethnic minority groups started to increase in 1978, when an Access course linked to the Primary B.Ed was established in conjunction with the then City and East London College (now City and

Table 1: Ethnic origin of 1st year B.Ed primary students 1991-1994

Ethnic Origin	1991	1992	1993	1994
English				
Scottish	54% (67)	63% (96)	52% (64)	57% (81)
Welsh				
Irish	7% (9)	2% (3)	7% (9)	5% (7)
Caribbean	23% (28)	20% (31)	12% (15)	14% (20)
African	7% (8)	3% (5)	5% (6)	6% (8)
Asian	6% (7)	3% (5)	8% (10)#	5% (7)#
Greek Cypriot &	2% (3)	4% (6)	3% (4)##	3% (4)
Turkish Cypriot				
Turkish	-	-	-	1% (1)
Latin American	-	-	-	1% (1)
Other	1% (2)*	5% (7)*	12% (15)**	8% (12)**
Don't Know	-	-	1%	
Total	100% (124)	100% (153)	100% (124)	100% (141)

Note:

Raw figures are in brackets

Different method of classification used as follows:

1991 & 1992 — classified by tutors

1993 & 1994 — self classification

Key:

* Included white European

** Included white European, and students of mixed ethnic origin (5 in 1993, 4 in 1994).

\# There were no Bangladeshi students in 1993, there was 1 in 1994.

\#\# There were no Turkish Cypriot students in 1993, there were 2 in 1994.

Islington College). It was one of the first courses to provide an entry to the teaching profession for applicants of African and Caribbean origin who did not possess the standard entry qualifications. In 1991 the School established a link with the College of North East London and developed an access course which specifically targets bilingual students.

The increase in the number of students from ethnic minority groups has had a significant effect in changing the ethos of the School. A strong commitment to anti-racist and multicultural education permeates all the

Table 2: UCAS Ethnic Monitoring Data for Applicants to Initial Teacher Training Courses in 1993

ETHNIC ORIGIN	Application rate (% of ALL applicants)	Admitted/Accepted (% of ALL applicants)	Admitted/Accepted (% of Ethnic Group)
Bangladeshi	0.2	0.1	29%
Chinese	0.1	0.1	52%
Indian	1.1	0.9	39%
Pakistani	0.8	0.7	41%
Asian other	0.4	0.4	49%
TOTAL ASIAN	2.6%	2.2%	40.5%
Black African	0.35	0.2	26%
Black Caribbean	1	0.9	39%
Black other	0.4	0.2	29%
TOTAL BLACK	1.8%	1.3%	34%
TOTAL WHITE	91%	92.5%	41%
Other	0.7	0.6	42%
Not known	3.55	3.2	43%

Source: UCAS 1993

work of the School. One of the effects of this has been to encourage an increasing number of standard entry applicants from ethnic minority groups.

Survey of Ethnic Origin and Languages Spoken

The School of Teaching Studies has been successful in widening access, but there was concern that some local ethnic minority groups were still under-represented in the School. The Language and Learning Project focused initially on a survey of the ethnic origin and languages spoken by first year students on ITT courses. This revealed that 31 different languages were spoken by the BEd and PGCE students in 1993, ranging from Arabic to Yoruba. The ethnic composition of first year BEd students at the School, from 1992 to 1994, is shown in Table 1 below. UCAS ethnic monitoring data for applicants to Initial Teacher Training courses nationally in 1993 is set out in Table 2.

Comparing the School's data with the 1993 UCAS data on national student intake to ITT courses, it is clear that the School recruits more Black and Asian students than in Higher Education overall. In 1993, 17% of students on the BEd course were of African and Caribbean origin, 8% were of Asian origin, and 14.5% were of Greek Cypriot, Irish and mixed origin. Just over half were white English, Welsh or Scottish. The UCAS data show that considerably less Black and Asian applicants were accepted on ITT courses nationally. White applicants made up 92.5% of the total number of applicants accepted, compared with only 2.2% of Asian applicants and 1.3% of Black applicants. The UCAS data also showed that the acceptance rates for Black applicants in 1993 were lower than for other ethnic groups — 34% of all Black applicants were accepted compared to 40.5% of Asian applicants and 47% of white applicants.

The School of Teaching Studies data for 1993 and 1994 revealed that whilst the School recruits students from a range of ethnic backgrounds, the following groups were under-represented: Bangladeshi, Hong Kong Chinese, Turkish Cypriot and Greek Cypriot. To encourage applications from these groups the Project team is building on links with local community groups. Members of the targeted groups have emphasised that the provision of language advice, guidance and support would be a major factor in their decision to apply for ITT courses at the School. As part of the campaign to attract applicants from these community groups, the Project team has produced a promotional leaflet which includes information on the provision of language learning workshops for bilingual students and speakers of Caribbean Creole languages.

Language Across the Curriculum

The importance of language and its role in widening educational opportunity has been the main focus of this Project. Work on language issues is relatively new in ITT and in higher education in general. However for well over a decade language has been the subject of debate, government reports, research and educational policy and practice in schools and further education colleges. (Department for Education and

Science 1975, 1981, 1985, 1988; Rosen and Burgess 1980; Nowaz 1984; Roussou 1985; Stubbs 1985; Khan 1985; Fitzpatrick 1987; Tansley 1986; Taylor 1987, 1988).

The Bullock Report, *A Language For Life* (Department for Education and Science 1975), laid the foundations for the development and implementation of language policies and practices in local education authorities, schools, further and adult education institutions. Its significance lay in the recognition of the importance of language for the educational progress of pupils, but in particular for speakers of languages other than English. The report highlighted the educational underachievement of 'immigrant children', particularly children of 'West Indian' origin, and the inadequacy of response to the needs of bilingual and bidialectical children.

> Immigrant children's attainment in tests and at school in general is related not only to language but several other issues, particularly those of cultural identity and cultural knowledge. No child should be expected to cast off the language and culture of the home as he [sic] crosses the school threshold, nor to live and act as though school and home represent two separate and different cultures which have to be kept firmly apart. The curriculum should reflect many elements of that part of his life which a child lives outside the school. (p. 286)

The Report had a significant impact on schools and it led to a number of developments: policies emphasising language across the curriculum; projects supporting bilingual children in their language learning and educational development (ILEA* Centre for Urban Educational Studies 1975-1978); and collaborative support for learning in the multilingual classroom (ILEA Centre for Urban Educational Studies 1984, ILEA Writing Project 1987); the Centre for Language in Primary Education (1988) developed a handbook for teachers, *The Primary Language Record* which included a focus on bilingualism.

In the further and adult education sector increased awareness of the importance of language for educational achievement led to innovative pedagogic approaches. Robson (1988) in *Language, Learning and Race* argued for and puts forward strategies for integrating English language support within the mainstream academic/vocational curriculum. The Inner London Education Authority's Language and Literacy Unit has been important in promoting the equality of 'access, opportunity and outcomes' in education. It brought together practising teachers to research and develop strategies and materials directly relevant to the language development of students from linguistically diverse backgrounds. Central to its work is a college-wide approach to language and the provision of language workshops for bilingual students (ILEA 1989).

Particularly influential was the work of the Afro-Caribbean Language and Literacy Project (ALLP) on language awareness, which originally focused on Caribbean language issues. It recognised that standard English as the language of education and authority is not the first language of the majority of students, and that most speak a regional variety of English or another first language. The ALLP argued that this linguistic diversity needed to be acknowledged and utilised. Central to the work was an anti-racist approach to language teaching and learning which focused on the relationship between power, language and identity. Placed within a historical, political and social context, it challenged taken-for-granted assumptions and attitudes about the status of standard English and other European languages, in comparison to African and Caribbean languages. The work of the ALLP led to two key publications: *My Personal Language History* (Harris and Savitzky 1988) which consists of individual language histories and experiences written by students; and *Language and Power* (ALLP 1990), a comprehensive collection of teaching and learning materials based on the belief that:

> ...a key part of the language curriculum for all students should be an outline of the social and political factors which helped determine the development of standard English. It is also necessary to make available to both students and teachers as much information as possible about languages in general and about the history and development of Caribbean Creole languages in particular. This includes an understanding of their grammatical structure, pronunciation patterns, vocabulary and idioms... Students' own knowledge and understanding of different languages and language varieties are an invaluable resource for language teaching. It is in this context that progress in the multilingual classroom can be achieved, not just for students of Caribbean origin, but for students of all races and backgrounds (p. v).

These developments represented a movement away from traditional approaches to language and its preoccupation with standard English conventions. It also challenged prevailing attitudes, which ignored and marginalised bilingual students' first language and failed to recognise the linguistic and educational diversity of students, thus contributing to their educational underachievement. Projects and developments such as these are only just beginning in the higher education sector. What language development and support is provided has tended to be primarily for students classified as coming from overseas and is often delivered in isolation from mainstream courses. So it was the work already undertaken in further and adult education that influenced the philosophy and practice of the Language and Learning Project at the School of Teaching Studies.

Language and Learning Project

* *Language learning workshops* were set up for bilingual students and speakers of Caribbean Creole languages on ITT courses. The programme included, amongst other elements, language awareness work. Workshops were immensely beneficial in developing students' linguistic, academic and professional skills. As a result students developed greater confidence and improved their communication skills, so were able to participate and contribute more to discussions and seminars. These were some of the comments that were collected from students as part of the evaluation of the workshops:

> The workshop has helped to boost my confidence considerably. Before coming to the workshop my self-esteem was very low due to problems with assignments. I had a lot of problems organising my work and was under a great deal of pressure. I'm more independent in my learning now.

> I attended the workshops because I needed some advice. Everybody helps each other at the workshop, it is not at all competitive. You feel that you can talk openly about aspects of the course which you are finding difficult. The fact that the guidance and support given is related to the course was very important.

> Since I have been to the workshop I feel that my language and culture are recognised and I feel a greater degree of confidence about being bilingual.

- *A staff development programme* was organised on 'Language Across the Curriculum', which all teaching and administrative staff in the School attended. Tutors reported that they found the sessions useful in allowing them to reflect on language and equal opportunities issues. They welcomed the opportunity to explore ways of putting into practice strategies for supporting bilingual students, in particular, how to utilise the linguistic and educational diversity of students in the planning and delivery of the curriculum and how to make explicit the academic and linguistic requirements of course work.

- *Learning and teaching materials* were produced. These include a collection of self-study language development materials ranging from: writing evaluations and reflections of teaching practice; planning and writing assignments; how to proof-read your work; summary of tenses; strategies for supporting bilingual students; writing curriculum vitae and supporting statements for jobs. A Learning Pack entitled *Primary and Secondary Education in England and Wales: Issues and debates*, was also produced. The pack is an invaluable source of information on developments in the Educational System. The sections on the National Curriculum were particularly beneficial: one Bangladeshi student on the primary PGCE course observed:

  > The pack is structured and written in an interesting way which is easy to follow for students like myself for whom English is a second language. It provided me with essential background information to the whole structure of the National Curriculum and what is demanded from schools, pupils and parents. All of this was new to me as I was educated in Bangladesh. The ideas I gained from the pack will be useful to me in my training here and in my career as a teacher.

  Although the materials and Learning Pack were produced primarily for bilingual students and students whose educational experience is outside England and Wales, feedback shows that the materials have been useful to all students.

  As the Project developed it became clear that there were two other important areas that needed to be considered which had not been identified in the original objectives:

120

- *The BEd selection and admissions procedures* indicated that bilingual students were disadvantaged by some aspects of the selection procedure.

  Some applicants had been rejected on the basis of their written language in the entry assignment. This was despite giving a good interview performance, demonstrating a real commitment to teaching and a realistic perception of teaching in inner-city schools. The provision of on-course language support workshops has made it possible to accept more bilingual and bidialectical students.

  A group activity exercise used as an icebreaker as part of the selection procedure appeared to disadvantage bilingual students. This has been changed so as to be less culturally specific and structured to encourage participation by all applicants. Admission criteria have been reviewed to avoid possible bias. Specific questions on equal opportunities and multicultural education have been included in the interview schedule, thus enabling candidates who have experience of and/or a commitment to equal opportunities issues, to discuss this at interview.

- *An ITT induction programme* was developed and focused on language across the curriculum and particularly the linguistic and cultural backgrounds of our students and the pupils they teach. This was a compulsory two week programme for all students, culminating in group projects on London's community groups, and an assignment on personal language history or on awareness of language issues in working with young children.

  The aims of the programme were:

  — to increase awareness of the linguistic diversity and history of London's communities;

  — to explore the struggles and contributions of individuals, groups and communities in overcoming inequalities;

  — to develop awareness of language issues through language awareness and personal language histories;

  — to gain an insight into how teachers can support bilingual children's language development;

The programme included visits to schools with well developed practice in multicultural and multilingual education, and lectures and seminars given by tutors and guest speakers representing local ethnic minority communities, on the following:

— world languages in London, the history of language education, and bilingualism;

— history and present day experience of London's ethnic community groups and refugee population;

— African and Caribbean story-telling.

The achievements of the programme are evident in the following comments from students:

> It increased my appreciation of the value which each culture has and the importance of recognising the mother tongue of bilingual children. It also made me want to look more into my own language and how it developed. I have become more aware of the struggles and hardship that different community groups encountered when they first arrived in this country. All this will help me a great deal in the classroom.

> I have gained a wider understanding of London's diversity. I learnt a great deal from other students on the course. As I can only speak one language, it was an eye opener to know that there are students on the course who can speak four languages. Being aware of issues to do with racism and sexism helps you look at things from a different perspective, which is important for becoming a teacher.

> Being of Asian origin I could relate to most of the issues mentioned. The course certainly made me feel much better about my language and cultural background in a 'white' society.

> I come from Africa, so I'm not originally an English speaker. This course gave me more confidence to say who I am, to fight against ignorance from people and myself toward other languages.

> I felt more able and proud to state my language and ethnic background to others and on forms.

The Way Forward

Language across ITT is an approach which places language at the centre of educational policy and practice. To ensure that language issues form an integral part of an institution's commitment to the equality of educational opportunities, an active language policy should be developed and implemented. This requires co-operation and liaison between language specialists and other specialist subject tutors.

The policy should include the following elements:

- A language co-ordinator and working party which have overall responsibility for co-ordinating and implementing the policy

- A system for reviewing and evaluating the effective implementation of the policy, with a yearly action plan

- A comprehensive system for monitoring students' ethnic origin and languages, progression rates, and reasons for withdrawal or failure. Action should be taken based on the outcomes of the monitoring

- Community outreach work targeted at under-represented groups to ensure recruitment from across all communities

- Admissions teams to ensure that selection and recruitment procedures do not disadvantage bilingual and bidialectical students

- A programme of staff development that entails an examination of the linguistic and cultural backgrounds of students, language issues that affect the students' performance, and strategies for better supporting their language development

- The planning and delivery of the ITT curriculum to include a 'Language Awareness' programme reflecting the linguistic, cultural and educational diversity of students

- Course teams who analyse the linguistic skills a student requires for entry to the course and the successful completion of the course

- The linguistic and academic requirements of courses to be made explicit and discussed with students. These are to be developed and learned in an integrated and contextualised way as part of the curriculum

- First year ITT courses to have a language and study skills component as part of the curriculum

- Language learning workshops to be provided for all students who require it. These should cater for individual language development in the context of mainstream course requirements.

The School of Teaching Studies has moved some way towards implementing the above elements. An evaluation of The Language and Learning Project has shown that the work of the Project benefits not only bilingual students and speakers of Caribbean Creole languages but, indeed, all students. The knowledge, skills and experience that students have gained from this innovative approach to language across ITT has also enabled them to incorporate aspects of language in the planning and delivery of the school curriculum, thereby providing greater equality of educational opportunity for all children in classes where they are teaching.

* ILEA: Inner London Education Authority serving the twelve inner London boroughs, abolished by the Conservative government in 1990.

Bibliography

Centre for Language in Primary Education (1988) *The Primary Language Record: Handbook for Teachers*, London: ILEA/CLPE.

Department of Education and Science (1975) *A Language for Life* (The Bullock Report), London: HMSO.

Department for Education and Science (1981) *West Indian Children in Our Schools* (The Rampton Report) London : HMSO

Department for Education and Science (1985) *Education for All* (The Swann Report), London: HMSO

Department for Education and Science (1988) *Report of the Committee of Inquiry into the Teaching of English Language*, (The Kingman Report). London: HMSO

Department for Education and Science (1988) *English for ages 5-11* (The Cox Report), London: HMSO

Fitzpatrick, F. (1987) *The Open Door*, London: Multilingual Matters.

Khan, V. S. (1985) *Education for all. Chapter 7 of the Swann Report*, Working Paper No. 6, London: Centre for Multicultural Education.

Harris, R. and Savitzky, F. (1990) *My Personal Language History,* London: New Beacon Books/ALLP.

ILEA Afro-Caribbean Language and Literacy Project (1990) *Language and Power,* London: Harcourt, Brace, Javanovitch.

ILEA Centre for Urban Educational Studies (1984) *Collaborative Learning: Examples of How Collaboration Supports Learning in the Multilingual Classroom*, London:ILEA

ILEA Language and Literacy Unit (1989) *Aspects of Language Across the College,* London:ILEA.

The National Writing Project (1987) *Working with Bilingual Writers 3-16*. London: ILEA

Nowaz, H. (1984) *Teaching Bengali as a Mother Tongue in Britain: A Teacher's Bilingual Guide*, London: Schools Curriculum Development Committee/ Schools Council Publication

Robson, M. (1987) *Language, Learning and Race*, London:Longman/FEU

Rosen, H. and Burgess, T (1980) *Languages and Dialects of London's School Children*, London: Ward Lock Educational.

Roussou, M. (1985) *Teaching Greek as a Mother Tongue in Britain: A Teacher's Bilingual Guide*, London: Schools Curriculum Development Committee/Schools Council Publication.

Stubbs, M (1985) *The Other Languages of England*, London: Linguistic Minorities Project/Routledge and Kegan Paul.

Tansley, P. (1986) *Community Languages in Primary Education: Report from the Schools Curriculum Development Council*, London: Mother Tongue Projects/NFER-Nelson.

Taylor, M.J. (1987) *Chinese Pupils in Britain: A Review of Research into the Education of Pupils of Chinese Origin*, Windsor: NFER-Nelson

Taylor, M.J. (1988) *Worlds Apart*, Windsor: NFER-Nelson.

SECTION IV
Managing effective change

Raising the Profile of Teaching as a Career
in schools and the community

Amar Khela with Mary Morrison

The shortage of Black teachers is a long-standing problem. The Swann Report of 1985 highlighted a serious shortage of entrants to teacher training from Black and Asian groups and commented on the problems associated with their recruitment. Despite various research projects and positive action initiatives, the 1994 Report by UCET (Universities Council for the Education of Teachers) revealed that a similar shortage continues to exist:

> Teaching continues to be less popular with ethnic minorities. Only 2.9% of Asian applicants and 4.4% of Black applicants preferred teacher training over other subjects, in comparison with 8.7% of white applicants. (UCET, Annual Report Second Series No.1 Summer, p.5)

Project Aims

The one year project, 'Teachers for the Future,' based within the School of Education at Huddersfield University (with Amar Khela seconded as the Project Director) had the following aims:

- to further race equality in the critical area of the recruitment, education and professional success of ethnic minority citizens within the teaching profession and to survey school students' perception of teaching as a career

- to heighten an awareness of these issues as an institution by gathering the experiences of existing Black students; auditing and reviewing current practice;

- The possible development of some form of modular provision/intensive Post Graduate Certificate in Education to allow ethnic minority students to convert or update other qualifications to achieve qualified teacher status. This chapter focuses on the work done as part of the first aim. Our other chapter discusses work done in relation to the other aims.

Numerous studies have researched the reasons why teaching is not an attractive option for Black and ethnic minority people, and this is confirmed by Shukla Dhingra and Kenny Dunkwu's report in Chapter 2 of this book. We decided to combine the research with a positive approach and developed a package for schools, organised a Taster course for the community at large and provided ongoing support and advice for anyone interested in training to be a teacher. This chapter outlines each of the above approaches and discusses some of the outcomes.

Work in schools

We felt that it was important to raise the profile of teaching as a career for all pupils and because recruitment begins in schools, we targeted 14-16 year olds who would be at the crucial stage of beginning to think about subject and career choices. The package was carefully developed to give useful information about entry qualifications, training, salary and careers structures as well as to gather data on students' perception's of teaching as a career. The package included:

- semi-structured discussions about teaching as a job with groups of 4-8 ethnic minority pupils
- questionnaires completed by the whole class
- workshops with the whole class, in which a video was shown of ethnic minority teachers talking about their careers, and various group tasks.

The research took place in three high schools in Calderdale, Huddersfield and Dewsbury. The cohort consisted of 200 Year 10 pupils who identified themselves as follows:

Ethnic Origin	Count	Percentage
African	4	2%
Arab	3	1.5%
Bangladeshi	4	2%
Caribbean	2	1%
Indian	16	8%
Pakistani	90	45%
English/ Scottish/ Welsh	81	40.5%

The overall term 'Black' is used for the first six categories of the pupils who constitute 59.5% of the sample and whose physical characteristics may lead to their encountering racial discrimination in society. Though not 'representative' in a strict statistical sense, these 200 pupils probably reflect the views and opinions of hundreds more.

Each of the schools had a different catchment area and there were some significant differences in the results of the research from each school, too.

School A draws its intake from a largely rural and 'commuting to Leeds/Manchester' professional white area. The 13% of ethnic minority population of the school represents a move by the Asian/Black community of a nearby town, a five mile bus journey away, to choose a comprehensive school for their children. This town is one of the few in the country to retain a selective system and these parents feel that the eleven plus exam too often resigns their children to secondary modern education. They also opt for this school positively because of its sixth form options.

131

School B is co-educational and comprehensive, serving pupils between the ages of 11-16. Out of the total number of 858 pupils, 56% are of Indian and Pakistani origin; 7% of African-Caribbean origin and 37% are white. This reflects both parental choice and local housing patterns.

School C is also co-educational and comprehensive, serving pupils between the ages of 11-16. Out of the total number of 693 pupils, 67% of the pupils are of Indian and Pakistani background; 2% are of African-Caribbean origin and 21% white. This too reflects both parental choice and local housing patterns.

Semi-structured discussions

The small group discussions provided qualitative data and also helped to identify the main areas to be researched. The pupils' concerns were mainly focused around issues of teacher expectations and teacher pupil relationships.

In School A there has been an Asian student teacher on placement and also a newly qualified ethnic minority teacher on a temporary contract. The ethnic minority students felt that although teaching is a 'good and respectable job' they would not choose it as a career option because of their own experience of racism amongst pupils and staff or because they had witnessed Black teachers being subjected to racism. Siraj-Blatchford (1991) too quotes the Swan Report of 1985 which 'cited racism in schools and the restricted career opportunities open to Black teachers as some of the problems associated with recruiting Black teachers.' (p.177). Some of the comments made by the students were:

Teaching is the worst job ever.

Most teachers are racist.

Black teachers get hell from the white kids.

Black teachers are better working with Black children.

The working environment is important and I wouldn't want to work in a school, especially in a secondary school.

In School B there are four Black teachers, one of whom is a senior teacher and one a classroom assistant. The discussion in School B was very different. There were some comments about teacher expectations in relation to particular teachers but the pupils generally had positive experiences of school and teachers. Some of the comments made were:

It feels good to see a Black teacher.

Some English people laugh at Asians. They don't like Asian teachers because they're racist. (These comments concerned the classroom assistant.)

It would be better if there were more Black teachers.

They might know what you feel, they might be able to help you with troubles at home because they know about the religion and culture.

The discussion concluded with the following dialogue:

Q. Why do you think there are so few Black teachers in schools?

A. They are probably trying to find some office jobs instead of working in schools.

Q. Why?

A. It is much easier.

Due to time restrictions, School C was involved only in completing the questionnaires.

Questionnaires

A questionnaire consisting of 78 questions and statements was then constructed, which covered topics relating to post-16 educational intentions; parental aspirations; attitudes towards teachers and teaching and perceptions of Black teachers drawing on some of the ideas in a similar survey carried out by Singh, Brown and Darr (1988). They were completed by the whole class during class time. The pupils were asked to tick a yes/no box or to indicate their level of agreement with each of the statements on a four or a five point scale. The questionnaires were administered to all the pupils in order to identify any commonalties or differences. The data was analysed in terms of category counts basic statistics. Correlation T-tests and F-tests were also applied to establish any statistically significant differences between groups.

Interestingly, on a number of issues the views of the white and Black respondents were very similar but there were also some significant differences between the two groups.

Aspirations

The majority of pupils have high aspirations and want to continue their education beyond school. Thirty percent would like to undertake training to do skilled work; 64% aspire to get a higher degree and hope to have a professional career. Only 6% of the total sample, half of them Black, are prepared to do unskilled or semi-skilled work. Most of the Black pupils were born in England and share many of the aspirations and interests of the pupil population at large. This evidence seems to contradict findings from earlier studies such as Beetham's study in 1967, Fowler, Littlewood, Madigan (1976), who drew 'attention to disparities in aspiration between immigrant and native school-leavers elsewhere.' (p.74) It is also probable that 'many of these pupils are coming to use academic qualifications as an essential defence against the discrimination they fear they will meet in the labour market.' (Eggleston *et.al.*, 1986)

Influence over choice of job/career

Contrary to popular belief, this research showed that there is evidently no conflict between the Black pupils' interests and what their parents want them to achieve. The pupils shared their parents' emphasis on the value of education. During discussions too, the pupils felt confident that their parents would ultimately support them in their choice of career.

Statistically significant differences exist between the Black pupils and the white in terms of the most influential person when choosing a job/career. 48% of the Black pupils and 60% of the white pupils are likely to be most influenced by their fathers. Furthermore, 45% of the Black pupils compared to 73% of the white would seek advice and information from their fathers. This difference may partly be due to the fact that some of the Black pupils know that their fathers may not be familiar with the systems here.

It is interesting that brothers/sisters, uncles/aunts and other relatives are other influential people for the Black pupils whereas the white students are much more likely to be influenced by their mothers, teachers/career advisors.

Important factors when selecting a career

Similar factors are important to both groups when selecting a career. Salary, job satisfaction, promotion prospects feature high on their list of priorities while social status and job security come at the bottom of the lists.

	Black pupils		White pupils	
	Count	Percentage	Count	Percentage
Nursery	72	61%	38	47%
Interest in teaching in particular age group				

A significantly higher proportion of Black pupils would like to teach in a nursery compared to their white colleagues. Discussions during the workshops revealed that the majority of pupils believed that working with young children would be an easy option. During the small group discussions with the Black pupils, the general impression was that racism is less prevalent in the nursery and that bilingual teachers are needed to support the learning of young children.

The least desirable option amongst both groups is to work in a secondary school. The second most desirable option is to work in an infant school. There is interest in working at a university too, probably because of the perceived status.

	Black pupils		White pupils	
	Count	Percentage	Count	Percentage
School A	0	0%	8	28%
School B	5	34%	2	28%
School C	64	79%	16	59%
Interest in becoming a teacher				

It is interesting that none of the Black pupils in School A were interested in going into teaching. Pupils in School B had fairly clear ideas about the kind of areas that they wanted to go into after leaving school. Significantly high percentages of pupils overall were interested in teaching in School

C. It was unfortunate that the short time-scale of one year prevented us from doing any other work in School C.

Attitudes towards teaching

The general impression amongst both groups was a favourable one and responses to one of the seven statements in this section revealed a significantly more favourable attitude amongst Black pupils. Fifty nine percent of the Black pupils compared to 52% of the white pupils considered teaching to be a rewarding job.

An unexpected finding was that the demands and stresses of teaching must be evident to most pupils, since only two pupils, both white, out of the total sample thought that teaching was easy work.

The proportion of unsure responses to statements such as 'Teaching is well paid' and 'Teaching is a dead end job' may suggest that perhaps the pupils do not have sufficient knowledge about the job, its salary structures and its career prospects.

Opinions about whether teachers should be able to speak some of the community languages other than English revealed significant differences: 79% of the Black pupils shared this view, as did 50% of the white pupils.

	Black pupils		White pupils	
	Count	%	Count	%
My parents would like me to become a teacher	31	26%	18	22%
Not sure	58	49%	36	44%
Parents' attitudes towards teaching				

Although Black parents appeared to be slightly more in favour of teaching, an unusually high number from both groups were unsure about their parents' attitude towards teaching as a career.

Attitudes towards Black teachers

Responses to the section on Black teachers reveal some of the most significant differences in the perception and attitudes between the two groups.

	Black pupils		White pupils	
	Count	%	Count	%
More Black teachers are needed Strongly Agree	97	82%	33	41%
Not sure	16	13%	28	35%
Black teachers would help to reduce prejudice Strongly Agree	91	76%	30	37%
Not sure	21	18%	21	26%
Black teachers encourage Black pupils to perform better Strongly Agree	67	56%	26	32%
Not sure	36	30%	30	37%
Black teachers would be resented by white pupils Strongly Agree	41	34%	19	23%
Not sure	42	35%	31	38%
Opinions about Black teachers				

This then was the situation we found, one that we believe could well be replicated across the UK. The remainder of the chapter describes the initiatives that succeeded in attracting more young people from ethnic minority groups into teaching.

1. The Workshops

These involved the whole class and the teachers. We explained to the students what our research project was about with a hand-out which included suggestions for follow-up work (see Appendix 1). Each workshop consisted of a fifteen-minute video showing Black teachers talking about their career, followed by two group tasks. Both proved very useful when I was working in schools and with the community.

After watching the video, which is described more fully below, the pupils worked in small groups to sort a set of ten printed statements. The statements were to do with entry qualifications, training, the job, career prospects and salary structures. The sharing at the end generated a lot of discussion and provided an opportunity to give information in an interesting way. Some of the information offered seemed to surprise the pupils — for example they were amazed that the salaries could be so high at the top end of the scale.

The second task required the pupils to list the qualities of a good teacher, and then to rank them. According to the pupils, a good teacher is:

Friendly

Fair and treats everyone the same

Understanding

Patient

Good at her/his subject

Interesting and enthusiastic

Firm with the pupils

Genuinely interested in children

The pupils seem to have ideas about what the ideal teacher should be and are well able to appraise the effectiveness of those they know.

2. The Video and Booklet: Teaching as a Career

The video was specially made for our purpose. It was intended to provide positive Black role models and to highlight different entry routes into teaching and to describe progression routes and different aspects of the job. As part of my role as project worker, I had interviewed seven teachers working in infant, junior and secondary schools. I asked them all the same questions, on a structured framework (see Appendix 2) then carefully edited the discussions to produce this 15-minute video and an accompanying booklet, entitled 'My Career as a Teacher.'

I include some samples of transcript from this booklet. First, a newly qualified teacher, Sharia Azhar, reporting on her experience during first temporary appointment at primary school in Dewsbury:

When I started to teach in schools, I felt as though I was doing something useful right from the first day. I was helping children who could not communicate in English. I had been given the impression that Asian parents do not care much about their children's education; contrary to that, I found that they were very interested. They just did not have access to the information they wanted or needed because of language barriers. Parents often do not have the confidence and feel embarrassed to come forward to ask questions about their child. This was where I could help. So helping the parents and the children, working with both, I found that I was doing something useful and on a day to day basis I could see that I was helping to make a difference in the school where I work.

Once parents realise that you are a teacher that immediately gives you the status, and that you are willing to help, they do seek you out. I have helped to develop good relationships with parents and we have set up various workshops to raise the parents' awareness of what happens in school and to give them practical ideas on ways of supporting their children's learning.

Dorothy Smith, the headteacher of a primary school in Batley, describes the reasons for her progression within her career.

Once I decided that I wanted to be a teacher and went through the school system I naturally went on to train as a teacher and became one. I suppose choosing teaching as a career came once I started to teach. When I got my first job, I realised that schools made a difference and I wanted to be a part of making that difference. I also realised that I needed to be somewhere in the decision-making of the school to have some influence. 1 very quickly made up my mind that I needed to get on in my career to begin to make a real difference.

She also demonstrates the challenges and delights of the profession:

The key aspect that I found most rewarding as a teacher was working with the children. I think they are an inspiration, and are always bringing things for you and they remind you of the newness of things. When you are getting fed up, depressed or when you think life has nothing to offer, the children will always remind you that life is important. As a head teacher I have enjoyed working with teachers in a similar sort of way. I enjoy working with people as I enjoy the interaction, and all the challenges that it brings. It does not mean that it is all pleasant but I do enjoy the challenge of working through things with adults, just as a teacher I enjoyed working through things with children.

Pushpa Prabakhar, now an advisory teacher in Bradford, indicated the strength and determination she needed to requalify to become a teacher in England:

> I did my B.Ed (Bachelor of Education) degree in India and did some teaching too. When I came here and explored the possibility of teaching, I found that my qualification and experience were not recognised.

> I started by working as a nursery nurse for a number of years. Eventually, I was able to do a one year PGCE course. Since then, I have worked hard and have obtained a Masters degree from York University by studying part time.

Pat Sarathy, a deputy head of a High School in Huddersfield, describes the route he chose towards his successful promotion:

> My first job was in a secondary school in Manchester. I was a member of the English department and had the responsibility for the library. I thought that I needed to be in a fairly senior position in order to really make changes within a school. I decided that if I was going to be the head of an English department then I would need to have a strong background in theatre or educational drama. I got a secondment to go to a drama college and enjoyed the course very much and got involved in dancing. So after some time, I applied for advisors' jobs and got one in Kirklees. I thought I could practice, visit schools and influence policy but it was not at all like that and I missed the children. I left the advisor's job and went back to teaching in a High School within a very rich multicultural area.

He also offers valuable advice on what qualities you need to be a teacher:

> The rewarding thing about school is not just the interaction with the children, or the way you see children growing. If you are on the sentimental side and think 'I love kids,' you are in for a shock. You have to be committed. It is hard work because children do not grow the way you want them to. It is not the teaching that matters as much as the learning. To me learning is infinite as well as exploratory. You build on what you learn. Relationships are very important because you have to relate to children genuinely. As a teacher you need the commitment. Your commitment must be to say 'I am going into

teaching to make sure everyone develops to their capacity.' Life is a continuous education. The nice thing about teaching is to make it terribly simple and working hard at making it simple.

If you want to go further in your career, you need to look at your qualities. You are not born with them. You need to look at things and find out where you want to go and within what time frame. Then set a business plan of how you are going to get there and work for it

Faz, a teacher in a primary school in Batley indicated the importance of the careers service in directing him towards the profession.

I always wanted to be a writer but the careers teacher told me that there is not much call for writers and that it may not be easy to make a living out of it. She told me that I would be better off choosing another profession and discussed teaching as an option.

At first I thought that I would apply for a B.Ed course. Although I wanted to take on the training, I was not sure that I wanted to pursue teaching as a career. So I took the option of doing a separate degree and a teaching qualification. I did a degree in English and a separate teaching qualification because of the doubts I had. It was during my final teaching practice when I actually made the decision to go into teaching. The training is not too difficult. You have to believe in yourself and be determined. I got a job in the school where I was doing my teaching practice.

Through all these very positive accounts of teaching as a career, the ability to forge the type of relationship with pupils mentioned by the children in the schools where we worked is most apparent.

Once I started to teach, I developed a relationship with my first class and realised that I really enjoyed teaching. I enjoyed it so much that I have never looked back. The sense of satisfaction that you get from developing a relationship with the children is a unique feeling. The job itself is demanding and you have to be committed to get the most out of it.

We were also fortunate in that many of these teachers were able to act as positive role models for the intending teachers as part of our Taster Day programme.

3. The Taster Course

This was jointly funded by the Department for Education and Kirklees and Calderdale Training and Enterprise Council (TEC). A particular feature of our programme was the funding of ethnic minority teacher mentors by TEC to receive accreditation for their work at Master's level by following our 'Mentoring in the Workplace' Module. Twenty one of the 31 participants who attended the Introductory Day were mentored by ten Black mentors when they visited schools.

Publicity

The publicity was targeted at:

* Black graduates currently unemployed or working below their employment status who might be interested to make a career change;
* 3rd year students at the university who might be interested in taking a shortage subject course; bilingual workers in schools in Kirklees and Calderdale;
* institutions offering access courses, and
* sixth form students at selected schools. The course was also advertised on local Asian radio as well as in the local papers and in the councils' vacancy bulletin.

The course consisted of an introductory day, work-shadowing programme in schools and follow-up days at college. The aims of the course were to:

* show a range of entry routes into teaching and to illustrate the opportunities for career progression
* provide information about entry qualifications, training, student grants and loans
* introduce the National Curriculum
* provide guidance on application procedures, including compiling a curriculum vitae, writing letters of application and planning for interviews
* provide a work-shadowing programme in schools with Black teachers, where possible.

Several of the mentors were the same teachers that took part in the video. The participants found the involvement of Black mentors very useful. Here are some of the comments:

Having a Black mentor who understood me helped.

Felt comfortable to ask questions.

Gave insight into what is taught and ways of teaching.

Interesting to observe class organisation and the relationship between teachers and students.

Several mentors mentioned that they felt that they had benefited from the opportunity to reflect on their own practice, and that they had a more sophisticated awareness of what the role of mentor entailed.

The project as a whole generated huge interest. We ended up holding a large number of individual guidance and advice sessions. It is clear that there is genuine interest in teaching amongst the ethnic minority groups and it is up to the institutions to formalise procedures and to target local community groups. What is needed are networks and partnerships with Black teachers and Black parent groups. We found the production of the video, the newsletter, the taster course, the mentor scheme and workshops in schools, useful ways of forging links with the community, Black teachers and schools. However, this kind of 'one off' initiative does not cater for the real continuing need. As argued by Siraj-Blatchford (1991), Singh (1988) and Klein (1993), school experience plays an important role in a student's chances of achieving higher education. The successful encouragement of students from ethnic minority groups would have a significant and long term effect on the education system as a whole. This can be done through exposing them to successful role models, making links with families, ensuring that teachers and institutions are seen as partners and by getting schools to take part in student tutoring schemes and mentoring initiatives.

While some of the findings of this project have challenged certain assumptions, others have replicated the findings of previous enquiries concerned with the under-representation of minority ethnic communities in teaching. Although statistics help to point up questions and areas requiring further investigation, one year research projects are both limited and limiting in what they can achieve in terms of institutional changes. It is obvious that there are several areas where further work could profitably be undertaken. Teacher training institutions need longer-term funding in order to put into action programmes which will act as bridges and access routes for those who have been failed by the school system or do not have the required entry qualifications. Our next chapter discusses ways of successful intervention.

Bibliography

Eggleston, J., Dunn, D. and Anjali, M. (1986) *Education for Some.* Stoke, Trentham Books

Klein, G. (1993) *Education Towards Race Equality.* London: Cassell.

Singh, R. (1988) *Asian and White Perceptions of the Teaching Profession.* Bradford and Ilkely College.

Siraj-Blatchford, I. (1991) *A Study of Black Students' Perceptions of Racism in Initial Teacher Education.* British Educational Research Journal Vol 17, No. 1.

Universities Council for the Education of Teachers. (1994) Annual Report Second Series No. 1

A video titled 'My Career as a Teacher' is available from: Teachers for the Future Project, The University of Huddersfield, School of Education, Holly Bank, Lindley, Huddersfield HD3 3BP

Appendix 1

Teachers for the Future Project

Help us with our research project — you can be researchers too!

We are interested in your views of *teaching as a job* — tell us what you really think.

We will be working with you to get responses to our video and to collect your ideas.

Our project is specifically about trying to encourage more Black teachers to join the profession, so we are also interested in your ideas about this.

Your GCSE work in English and Drama can also show us your ideas; there are some suggestions for the kinds of follow-up work you might discuss with your teachers on the next sheet.

Oral Work

You might choose to brainstorm your ideas and record them for us on a large sheet of paper, or directly onto tape or videotape.

Role Play

You might like to work in pairs or threes to show a variety of typical teacher and student situations. When you have developed your ideas you could tape or videotape your role-plays or develop them into a written script.

Drama

You might like to develop in pairs or threes an improvisation which tries to demonstrate the difficulties of teaching as a job. Your work here should explore what you see as fair and unfair ways in which teachers and school students behave. (Again if you were able to script or video these, we would be interested.)

Writing

There are many ways in which you might choose to write about teaching as a possible job — and it will be up to you to choose the style that you feel comfortable with.

(Some suggestions only: poems or short essays such as ' The teacher that I like would be...',

'What I like or dislike about teachers.'

'What I think your project should do to recruit more Black teachers')

But please do not use the names of any real teachers!

Appendix 2

Ingredients That Make a Good Teacher

The qualities that the students seek in their teachers in order of preference are:

1. Friendliness
All the pupils like teachers to be friendly, easy to get along with and have a 'good personality'.

2. Fairness and a sense of equality
The second most important quality is fairness. They would like teachers to treat everyone with the same respect. All pupils ought to be given equal attention, help and encouragement.

3. Understanding
An understanding of the difficulties that the pupils can face in and out of schools is felt to be important. Teachers should be reasonable in their expectations of the pupils.

4. Patience
The teachers need to be patient in order to work with the pupils. They should be calm, even tempered and unflappable.

5. Knowledge of subject
A good knowledge of subject is considered to be important.

6. Interest and enthusiasm
Teachers should not be only good at their subject but be able to generate interest and enthusiasm through the use of original and interesting ways of teaching.

7. Firmness
Teachers should be able to maintain discipline while remaining calm and "unflappable".

8. Likeness for children
Most pupils feel that a teacher should like children and there should be mutual respect between teacher and pupil.

Chapter 9

A Few Timely Sparks
Raising awareness in Teacher Training Institutions

Mary Morrison with Amar Khela

Most teachers and educationalists still fail to appreciate the effects of racism and sexism and, perhaps more seriously, they often fail to recognise it. They certainly fail to understand their own role in dismantling racism and sexism and the urgency of the matter.
(Iram Siraj-Blatchford, 1993, p.4-5).

Recognising the barriers

In using a case-study approach, one which draws upon the experience of students — ethnic minority and white — during their PGCE or 2 year shortage subject B.Ed teacher training at Huddersfield, as well as experience gathered from those who enrolled on our programme of Taster Days in the autumn of 1994, we recognise that any inferences we may draw will reflect only our local communities and the context of one initial teacher training institution. How far these can be generalised across to other institutions is problematic; nonetheless, those of us from nine or ten institutions who met regularly throughout 1994 to discuss issues arising from our one year 'Widening of Participation in ITT by Minority Ethnic Students' projects, tended to agree informally that certain key areas of entitlement emerged as main concerns and were common to us all. These were issues of access, qualifications, application and interview procedures, forms of on-going support or mentoring for students (particularly with curriculum content and organisation, school place-ments, language and learning needs, and profiling), career guidance and monitoring of progression.

Evidence gathered at different stages of the project indicated that there were discrete forms of cultural stereotyping in operation which those responsible for these processes in the institutions might need to become more open to and that sensitive whole institution staff development was urgently needed. We are confident that institutions which are prepared to tackle these issues will be addressing the concerns that lie at the heart of 'quality' assurance and auditing.

This chapter uses vignettes of student experience in order to try to map out some suggestions for staff development and/or quality guidelines and recommendations for our own and perhaps other HEIs. The recent framework offered by the Commission for Racial Equality, which offers five levels of institutional effectiveness across a range of operations, might also act as a useful guide to institutions wishing to develop quality procedures and practices.

By using student voices, perceptions and experiences gathered during our project to suggest important areas for change, we hope this may be seen as the first stage of an extensive process of dialogue and consultation, where those with management and other responsibilities engage in careful 'listening' to the Black student experience. This might be a useful and critical way of influencing and developing the implementation of equality of opportunity practices as part of the persistent struggle towards an organisational excellence which questions values and purposes, and recognises the social, political and economic contexts which affect both quality and equality.

Conjunctive relations as a way of learning

In his extended discussion of radical empiricism in his introduction to *Paths Towards A Clearing,* social anthropologist Michael Jackson suggests that, as researchers we need to move beyond the 'observer' position, characterised by what he terms the 'spectator' theory of knowledge:

> Unlike traditional empiricism, which draws a definite boundary between observer and observed, between method and object, radical empiricism denies the validity of such cuts and makes the *interplay* between these domains the focus of its interests.

The methodology he offers advocates the study of what William James termed 'conjunctive relations', that is the means whereby we try to reach into experiences which may be alien to us, in order to begin to perceive the connections between cultures. George and Louise Spindler (1982) and George Spindler (1987) echo this by stressing that educators need to engage in 'reflective cultural analysis' if they are to be able to begin the delicate processes of becoming aware of their own unconscious biases and cultural ethnocentrism. We suggest that it is here, in this critical hinterland, that staff development activities may need to lie, if the many barriers to progress perceived by our Black and ethnic minority students, both intending and current, are to be recognised rather than denied. Listening and opening ourselves to the realities of the voices speaking here may well lead to policy and practical changes that will benefit all students. (The first steps we have taken as an institution have taken the form of staff discussion with the whole team of initial teacher trainers based around the students' statements.)

The management of change, and the modelling of the processes that enable it, form the backcloth to this study. Fullan and Hargreaves (1992) p.122 offer similar strategies, suggesting that what they term 'process visions' need to be built up by more collaborative inclusive structures within educational institutions. They recognise the initial conflict which 'the articulation of different voices may create', but indicate the important gains an institution can make by confronting and working through such difficulties. They see this as part of the collaborative process, a valuable form of 'interactive professionalism'.

Across the world today, we see people profoundly dissatisfied with the institutions which dominate their lives... and teachers should be dissatisfied with their schools and their systems. It may only take a few timely sparks to create the momentum for radical change. ...Administrators should be looking for and supporting these kinds of positive pressure points in helping to bring about reforms in institutions.

Project Aims

Our other chapter on school students' perceptions of teaching as a career (Chapter 8) looks at that part of the first aim, while this chapter focuses on the second and some aspects of the third. Qualitative and quantitative data were gathered by us, with the invaluable assistance of Hala Seliet. Her M.Ed study of student and staff perceptions was commissioned by the project and offered significant insights. We also drew on a final PGCE project by Zahida Rashid which looked at the needs of local bilingual teaching assistants and instructors, and documented on video some of the concerns and successes of current ethnic minority students. This video, 'Destination Teaching', is intended for departments in our university whose students can transfer to our ITT degrees after two years.

The students' voices or descriptions of their experiences, are printed in italics and could be used in conjunction with the CRE framework and/or the NAFE Guidelines for needs analysis, action planning and monitoring as part of workshop activities for staff development. Such workshops would need to be given status and time by the institution and be valued as an important exercise, if they are to be seen as integral to putting the whole ITT training and partnership with participating schools into operation. Their voices introduce each of the major issues that need to be tackled in order to attract and support ethnic minority students in teacher training. Discussion of each of these issues and specific recommendations follow.

1. Recruitment, access and admissions procedures

Sadly you will be in a minority here. Better recruitment is needed. Once enough students of a particular minority go through the system they will pioneer their own needs.

As this first voice indicates, the existing ethnic minority students feel under-represented on our course. It was for this reason that we made the bid for funding* (included as appendix 1) to find out how to improve matters. Much of this section draws upon the experiences of those who attended our Open Days and DfE/Kirklees and Calderdale TEC funded Taster Days. Currently our, ethnic minority representation on ITT is between 2-3% over the past five years, which does not adequately reflect the 13% of the local population.

Targeting and publicity

Articles about teaching as a career and advertisements should appear more in the community newspaper and magazines.

More ethnic minority students could be encouraged to enter the course by being interviewed and taught by ethnic minority staff. This course should do more about promoting other successful Black ethnic minority teachers from a range of backgrounds.

Points to consider

- the recruitment of Black ethnic minority teachers to the course team.
- new publicity material clearly indicating the pathways and routes to gaining qualifications.
- strategic positioning of information in appropriate community gathering places, local radio and newspapers.
- the development of a network of community members working in teaching, who are prepared to give advice to those interested in finding out more, and clearly identified in our promotional materials.
- meetings with local community groups to raise the profile of teaching as a career.

Amar Khela's video, 'Teaching as a Career', described in Chapter 8, and her short leaflet of biographical details of local ethnic minority teachers

151

in a range of schools and career stages, from newly qualified to headteacher, present teaching as a career in a very positive and encouraging way.

Main recommendation

White monolingual staff with responsibilities for marketing institutions need to network with identified members of the surrounding community to develop more understanding of how their local community groups access information, consulting and working with them to establish the most efficient means of communicating.

2. Creating access, acknowledging existing qualifications

Prospective students should visit schools to find out as much as possible about education from the teacher's perspective — including their views on minority ethnic role models

It is important to shop around and find a course that fits your requirements

Check on the help you will gain and the attitudes of staff

Do you mean to tell me that the part-time degree I have been following in Combined Studies for six years will not equip me to teach a subject by following a PGCE because I have not studied enough of any one subject? Why have I been so wrongly advised? What can I do now? I have been teaching Urdu in British Schools at Instructor Level for fifteen years, I have degrees in Mathematics and Engineering from Pakistan. I cannot afford to stop working to support my family. How long is it going to take me to get the necessary qualifications?

As a result of special funding from the School of Education for targeted advertising to local community groups before our University Open Day in June 1994 and as a formal part of the programme on our Taster Days, the project became an unofficial advice and consultation centre for questions of access and qualifications for the rest of its duration. Although Amar is no longer in post, we have had 200-300 requests for assistance with complicated cases such as the one above. This was an unexpected area of work, and one which indicates clearly to us that much still needs to be done if the many ethnic minority teachers already working in our schools at the assistant or instructor level, are not to be trapped and remain perpetually within this sub-class. Each case was extremely time-consuming and often challenged our resources; it was frustrating to be able to offer so little, but the suggestions we make derive directly from this casework.

We were given extra funding by the Kirklees and Calderdale TEC for participants to 'work-shadow' ethnic minority teachers as part of our Taster Day programmes, because one of their priorities was for us to try to attract more of the significant pool of ethnic minority graduates who were either unemployed or working in jobs in our area that were well below their employment status.

Points to consider

* appointing an ethnic minority advice worker to the School of Education Registry to handle the complicated enquiries we as a project tried to handle and to influence the shape of the admissions process.

* urging the institution to become more autonomous, as is its right, in its recognition of qualifications from overseas. Currently, degrees either in main subjects or in education from many so-called developing countries are apparently rated by the British Council as of 'A' level equivalence, yet the contents and knowledge of such programmes appear similar to our own, and are accepted as such in other European countries with pre-existing colonial links, such as France.

* greater flexibility and use of Accreditation of Prior Learning (APL), together with the appropriate guidance and support, for bilingual intending teachers. (There are many suggestions and useful models in Meena Wood's *APL and Bilingual Learners* (1995)) This would have resource implications in terms of lecturers' time, and funding.

* the establishment of a part-time pathway of 'conversion to B.Ed.' modules for those intending to gain QTS. Such a programme exists in our institution for FE. The CATE requirements should not make this impossible, although we would clearly need to bid in for a quota of our allocation of places on our existing courses. Similarly we would need a quota for a more flexible part-time/ 2 year PGCE.

Such courses would need to cater for two distinct client groups, those who are already employed in schools, and those who would need to be placed in schools, i.e. the more traditional students.

- Funding such enterprises is complicated and would depend upon local circumstances. There will be opportunities within the SRB for dynamic new partnership arrangements between LEAs, schools and HE institutions, but only if the latter are proactive to the extent of having flexible, modular pathways worked out in conjunction with their partners, based on detailed community need analyses, and validated well in advance.

- As project workers we found it difficult to make our voices heard in trying to establish new more flexible routes to QTS as a priority, in the complicated structures of the institution. Yet it could be precisely such innovative measures that would add value and quality to our ITT.

Main recommendation

It should be a priority to find the ways to alert our institution to the need to develop more flexible conversion/access to teaching modules, in partnership with LEAs, and local schools, that will allow teachers already in post and supporting themselves and their families to gain QTS through part-time in-service routes. Such processes could clearly apply to all non-teacher assistants and or instructors.

3. Application and interview procedures

(The interview experiences reported here are drawn from experiences at a number of ITT institutions, not just our own.)

> *There were some questions that he just threw at me and I was really shocked. He asked me some questions about my cultural background and I didn't know what to say... he asked 'Do you watch Indian films, listen to Indian songs?' I'm not going to stand in front of classes and tell them that I watch Indian movies. It was harsh, that was. I didn't really enjoy answering those questions.*

> *At ... X ... I don't think I was really prepared for the interview, because I hadn't known that they were going to ask me about language and literature, which we hadn't done on our access course. That's where I felt let down. At ... Y ... they didn't ask me about the language and*

literature. I was a bit more prepared there and my interview went really well.

I planned to keep the fact that I had a nine month old baby at the time secret but somehow, I don't know how, the interviewer found out and he asked me... 'Who's going to look after your daughter?' I was just shell-shocked... I might have been looked down upon because I was a woman, with a child, because the PGCE course is so demanding they might have thought I wasn't up to it... I just said I wouldn't let myself in for something I didn't think I could cope with.

Points to consider

- All the course requirements and some aspects of guidance as to what will be expected at the interview need to be provided at the application stage.

- It was appreciated that many of our subject tutors had offered pre-interview appointments for informal guidance before participants on our Taster Days decided to make an application. Six of these were subsequently recruited.

- It would be helpful to have more ethnic minority members on the interviewing panels, and more women.

- Tutors need more training in dealing with sensitive intercultural and gender issues if prospective students are going to feel welcomed by the institution and comfortable during the interview process.

- Care needs to be taken over the interpretation of references, which we have occasionally found to contain unfortunate and ethnocentric comments on individuals' identities and work. (One such recently criticised an African-Caribbean for frequently applying a culturally contextual reading of British texts.)

Main recommendation

Staff development is needed for monolingual teachers to increase understanding of the way that intercultural awareness might enhance the interview and refereeing process.

4. Guidance, mentoring and networking systems

Induction and the allocation of tutors

> *The big thing that struck me is that you need a lot of energy It's very demanding on you physically and mentally, you're under pressure nearly all of the time... we needed more preparation in how to cope with this... and how to deal with difficult students... and how to build up our own confidence... right from the start. The university induction was too factual... all they told you could have been written down. The school's induction was much more professional.*

> *There should have been more of a multi-ethnic perspective throughout the whole course. There was not a single mention of it during the induction period, although the majority of schools we use reflect the richness of our local communities. We were not informed of the Equal Opps policies and procedures, or told who we could go to if we had a problem.*

> *Individual tutors were welcoming and genuinely supportive and helpful, clearly aware of the issues...but not all... the kind of welcome you receive is more important than too much information in the early days... you need to feel that the tutors are approachable and that you can ask them anything in confidence and they will not look down on you... I found out later that my confidences had not been kept...*

Many of the students commented upon the importance of the induction period and it was obvious that they considered this period crucial in establishing the ethos of the course. Their suggestions have provided our institution with many challenging ideas, and argue for restructuring the first few days of the programme. We also spent a most valuable two days working with partnership school teachers, at their suggestion, on a student entitlement document, since this was an area that they felt we, as an institution, needed to develop and clarify, not only for the benefit of the students, but also for the partnership.

Points to consider

- Emphasis during induction should be on 'getting to know each other', team-building and on coping/counselling and/or self-awareness strategies.

- More sessions on raising awareness of the workings of schools, their pupils and the presence of partnership teachers during induction days.

- Key information and timetables for the year to be presented in a user-friendly, jargon-free form in a comprehensive student handbook.

- Policies and procedures for dealing with cases of racial harassment.

- Forms of assessment to be clearly shown, with all the assignment titles, criteria deadlines and tutorial support available in the student handbook.

- Choice over personal tutors — who should recognise religious and cultural requirements.

Main recommendation

Staff to work together to present a coherent picture of the course rather than a fragmented — or duplicated — one. It is vital to the students that they present a welcoming, enthusiastic and supportive ethos. Many of our students are mature and come from a wide range of family, professional, and community experience. This experience deserves to be recognised and valued by the course, and students made clear that this is a matter of mutual respect.

5. Curriculum content and organisation

The course needs more balance and variation in its content if it is to put many Black cultures into a positive context.

The timetable was so structured that we couldn't even fit in a workshop where you could all sit down and say well I encountered this problem and how did you handle it... I certainly gained more from discussions ... actually learning from other students how they handled certain situations

Ethnic minority and majority students were surprisingly similar in their observations and suggestions. Most of our partnership schools are multiracial and white students in particular felt at a loss with the range of skills they needed at once to cope effectively in the classroom. The white students seemed unaware of the importance of the linguistic and cultural role their ethnic minority colleagues could fulfil, and did not on the whole recognise their importance as role models. However they were aware of a continuum of attitude in partnership schools towards the learning and language needs of bilingual students. They reported that some schools approached these positively and holistically within the mainstream curriculum, allowing pupils access to all their languages, and using global approaches to the National Curriculum wherever possible, while other schools still viewed second language learners as 'problems' and offered little representation of their cultures or languages or precious little support. (As part of the observation for the university Language and Literacy Module one student shadowed a 'quiet' newcomer from Pakistan in year 9 for two days and found that not a single teacher or other pupil spoke to her at all during that period. She met up with another Year 9 Panjabi speaker during break periods, but no-one in that school had recognised that she needed most of all to be placed in a class with this other girl, who might have performed a valuable translating bridge for her.) We have summarised the key suggestions made by these students below.

Points to consider

- Students want more professional training early on, not merely in subject specialisms, but in understanding how the diversity in their own perceptions of themselves as learners and their differing approaches to learning mirror what they will find in the classroom.
- A coherent structure for the course, closely linked to the school-based experience, with continuity and progression clearly indicated in the student handbook, and understood by school mentors.
- More help with interpersonal skills and the use of counselling approaches in working with difficult pupils and colleagues.
- Fewer lectures and more information available as hand-outs and through more active learning methods through seminar and groupwork, so that the university work reflects more closely the best practice of school approaches to the National Curriculum

- Access to computers, workshops and other facilities at times which are suitable to those who have children, and who may not be wealthy enough to own word-processors. Students who are lone parents dislike the compulsory word-processing requirement of some assignments. (A loan-system of lap-tops would help here.)

Main recommendation

During course review, the concerns of all the students might be considered as part of a package of special measures the institution might take in order both to attract and retain more Black/ethnic minority students and to implement some of the key equality issues of concern to all students.

6. School placements

The tutors should let you know what you are letting yourself in for... you know... long hours, dedication. You've got to be motivated, enthusiastic and you've got to be able to stick with the behaviour of disruptive pupils.

Placements should be in multi-ethnic schools for Black students, and wherever possible where there are other Black teachers. Being the first woman Muslim teacher in an all-boys Catholic school for my first placement was very difficult for me.

I would have welcomed a placement in a local school so that as a female without my own transport I, and others, might not need to travel so far from home. I was given a poor placement first, but was promised a better one next time. I ended up being expected to travel four hours a day for the second.

A white pupil deliberately tried to get me into trouble by lying about the treatment of him by me... fortunately I was helped by supportive staff in the school and my personal tutor at the university whom I contacted that evening at home. If this had happened at the other school I would have dropped out straight away.

The task of organising placements in schools is unquestionably a difficult, time-consuming and problematic one, but the ethos of the school and the support, or lack by it, of school mentors was seen by all the ethnic minority students as critical to their success.

They felt that where there were whole-school policies which demonstrated sensitivity to the delicate issues of culture, race and gender, they managed better and were likely to feel more welcomed and understood. Placements in all-white schools, where they were the first ethnic minority teacher, were viewed as the most difficult, since they experienced particular forms of racism, often unintentional and unthinking, and isolation, with no-one who recognised what they were experiencing and with whom they might discuss things.

Points to consider

- Establishing a network of Black/ethnic minority mentors to support the school placements of ethnic minority students, wherever possible, and making sure that members of this network were consulted on all partnership matters and able to communicate with and help to train white staff as part of the partnership's anti-racist strategy.

- Care taken over mentor training of teachers in partnership schools, to ensure more parity of experience and awareness of cultural and religious needs.

- Making sure that white students should be entitled to teaching in at least one multi-ethnic school.

Main recommendation

Staff both in the university and the partnership schools to develop networking with ethnic minority mentors and more awareness of how the choice of placement school and effective support of the students can influence their progression and success.

7. Assessment and monitoring of progression with a secondary emphasis on second language and learning needs

I started off doing the PGCE in Secondary and then after six weeks, realising it wasn't the course that I really wanted to do, I changed to the FE PGCE. In the secondary I had to teach subjects related to Business and Economics, although I didn't really have any qualifications in this area. I thought, if this subject doesn't interest me, it's not going to interest the pupils. In FE I can specialise in Information Technology.

My mentor has a certain style and she likes training teachers to teach as she teaches. I have seen other teachers at the same school teach differently and I prefer that and I have just gone and done it. The only problem is she is assessing me on my competencies so that worries me.

As students, whether Black or white, we all recognise that in schools there is confusion over who is assessing what. And many of the schools take students from several universities... I am handing my competencies to my teacher at the school and I am not getting them back because she doesn't know how to assess them... I don't think it has been explained to her how we should be assessed.

When I was informed that I had failed a (university) subject assignment I was unsure as to how this affected my position on the course. I felt very uncertain about this.

When I learnt that I had failed an assignment, I found out that others who had failed had had letters from the university, and had been able to redo their essays, Why did I only find out about my marks by pressing for them and why was my essay sent to the external examiner so I could not rewrite it for the deadline of the exam-board?

It was the ethnic minority students who overwhelmingly reported their anxiety about methods of assessment, and occasionally unfair treatment, such as receiving very negative criticism about their practice teaching sessions, use of English and comments about their oral delivery. Several of them said that they felt they had to prove themselves twice as hard as the white students.

Points to consider

- Clarification of student handbook to indicate full course content and means of assessment/retrieval/referral processes.
- Adequate language and learning support right from the start built into the course, and available to all students.

- More tutorial time to be allocated within all courses so that tutors who have set assignments can be available for consultation at the drafting and redrafting stages.

- A modular approach with 'second chances' built in during the year, for students who may have uneven pressures or long distances to travel.

- Staff development throughout partnerships to eliminate bias where cultural or religious perceptions may affect the assessment process.

Main Recommendation

Resources should be allocated to the analysis and monitoring of the language and learning needs of bilingual students, so that appropriate tutorial advice, guidance and language support services can be made available to all students. This should be a priority.

Influencing systems, monitoring equality as a quality issue

Be aware that there aren't many minority ethnic students on this course.

In conclusion, and again taking up the points raised through the voices of our students, we hope their powerful and critical auditing of their own experience can be positively received as reflecting the first principles of quality assurance. If institutions are striving for continuous improvement — as we believe them to be — through looking at and documenting the requirements of their students, the next step must be to manage their courses in such a way that they will ensure a consistency of service and provision, which can be closely monitored and reviewed.

We need to improve the image of the teaching profession as a whole, through out society.

This student voice echoes the National Commission on Education's findings reported in 1994:

It is vital that we consider the long-term attractiveness of the profession and aim to draw on the widest range of talent and skills to staff the profession... The more attractive teaching is seen as a career

162

option, the more it will attract high quality potential teachers (p.206-7).

The Commission was critical of the Government for not having published statistics on ethnic minority teachers either in post or in training, since:

This failure prevents the profession and the public from having an accurate picture of the ethnic composition of the teaching force, from setting recruitment targets and from monitoring progress. (p.209)

The Commission suggests that much greater effort is needed to woo ethnic minority teachers into the profession and suggests that projects such as TASC should target their materials towards this group if they are to encourage 'a positive view' of the 'status and value of teaching'.

It is ironic that we had funding for only one year for the project. As project workers, we found that it took us a year to establish ourselves and for our work to gain hold within the institution and our partnership schools, another year was certainly needed to disseminate and affect some real change within the institution. The impact of having an ethnic minority senior lecturer available for a year gave a terrific boost to our intending and current ethnic minority students, but now that her secondment is over, we are not sure how long it will be until we have another. Nor should it stop at that. Just as the isolated ethnic minority student found it tricky to be in an all-white staffroom, our institution might need to be aware of the pressures that being the lone member of staff place upon such a representative. We hear this theme in the following student voices:

Basically just to take into consideration the barriers we face as Asians and Blacks, I mean most schools have predominantly white staff... we are going to have problems... We are not familiar with the European way of thinking and talking...we don't have that background. It can be a barrier sometimes when you're socialising with staff and tutors... and so on.

I felt I needed much more help with learning about the language and culture of schools and Britain.

The social, economic and political variables which form the complex contexts of employment and education lie beyond the scope of this chapter, but throughout affect our recommendations. Ramindar Singh, in his article, 'Ethnic Minority Experience in HE' (1990) suggests that the

163

barriers to teaching are greater because its institutional setting exposes students to racism, whereas:

> pharmacy qualifications like those in medicine, law and accountancy, offer more opportunities for self-employment and, thus, minimise the impact of racial discrimination on subsequent employment.

We feel it is up to all of us working in schools and their partnership HE institutions to assume responsibility, collectively and individually, for dismantling these hefty barriers; taking some of the steps argued for so eloquently by our Black and ethnic minority students, may help teaching to be seen as a more welcoming, prestigious, culturally aware and diverse profession.

> A quality teaching profession should not have barriers to entry for any group in society (National Commission Education, 1994, p.209).

Bibliography

Fullan, M. and Hargreaves, A. (1992) *What's Worth Fighting For in Your School?* Buckingham, Open University Press.

Jackson, M. (1989) *Paths Towards a Clearing.* Bloomington, Indiana University Press.

National Commission on Education (1993) *Learning to Succeed.* London, Heinemann.

Singh, R. (1990) Ethnic Minority Experience in Higher Education, *Higher Education Quarterly* 44 4. pp.344-359.

Siraj-Blatchford, I. (1993) *'Race', Gender and the Education of Teachers.* Buckingham, Open University Press.

Spindler, G. and Spindler, L. (1982) Roger Harker and Schoenhausen: From the familiar to the strange and back again', in Spindler G.(Ed), *Doing the Ethnography of Schooling,* New York: Holt Rinehart and Winston.

Spindler, G. and Spindler, L. (1987) 'Cultural Dialogue and Schooling in Schoenhausen and Roseville: A Comparative Analysis', *Anthropology and Education Quarterly* 18 1 pp.3-16

Wood, M. (1995) *APL and Bilingual Learners,* London, Routledge.

Chapter 10

Recommendations

An analysis throughout this volume reveals a number of problems that were inherent in the project design, and many of these problems were apparent in a number of the HEFCE projects. One project (perhaps understandably not reported on in this book), produced a 50% drop-out rate. We suggest that the money could have been better spent if the ITT institutions and the funding body had planned more carefully. Accordingly, we have made recommendations to (A) the Higher Education Institutions and (B) the Funding Bodies

(A) The Higher Education Institutions

Policy

i.   Any attempts to attract Black and ethnic minority students must be underpinned by an effective, established commitment to equal opportunities. An Equal Opportunities policy must be in place, clearly stated and widely publicised. Moreover, policy implementation should be monitored by management staff and students and the policy reviewed at regular intervals.

ii.   Staff should receive professional development training on issues of race, with immediate provision for those involved in selection and recruitment of students. This training should not be on the model of

165

'race awareness' but should rather clarify issues relating to racism, institutional and personal, and both should equip staff with an understanding that 'equal opportunities' is more than a matter of 'treating all our students the same'.

iii. If institutions are committed to attracting Black and ethnic minority students, they should reflect this in the ethnic composition of their staff. We found that the most effective projects ran in institutions where staff were ethically mixed and which already operated an EO policy in staff as well as student recruitment. Chapter 7 of this book is one such positive model.

iv. When Black and ethnic minority staff are in post, they should be assured of the same career progression opportunities as their white colleagues. They must be allowed to define for themselves the academic parameters of their own research. They should not be expected to carry the burden of dealing with all the racism that arises and should not be set up as 'role models'. This is not to say that they should not be directly involved, should they so choose, in policy development on equality issues, and in mentoring schemes for ethnic minority students.

v. Black and ethnic minority external advisers should be called upon in the short term for the following purposes:

- to support and prevent marginalisation of solitary or isolated ethnic minority staff
- to sit on staff appointment panels
- to contribute to EO policy review
- to sit on panels that deal with complaints of discrimination
- to act as mentors for ethnic minority students. The contribution of the CRE was noted in the project studies. Local communities and Black and ethnic minority staff from other HEIs could take on these crucial positions short term.

vi. All students should be expected to study issues of equality — particularly relating to race and gender — as part of their courses. This should not be optional, although we understand that in-depth studies may need to be so. However, we recommend that in all students' work, assessment should take account of the students' understanding of issues of equality and particularly its relevance to teaching.

vii. The curriculum and the resources should take account of race and gender and, where appropriate, special educational needs. Reading lists should include relevant materials, eg. the FEU's *Staff Development for a Multicultural Society.*

viii. Effective monitoring to include ethnic monitoring, should be carried out on students: their recruitment, retention, progression and final results.

viii. Mentoring programmes should be in place for all students and mentors should be of the same ethnic group as their mentees. A network of mentoring should be established for Black and ethnic minority students while they are on school placement.

ix Recruitment: active recruitment of Black and ethnic minority students to teaching could be made more effective by:

- establishing links with sixth formers in schools and colleges to give them a clear view of what teaching offers as a career

- offering taster courses to adult returners

- access courses could be provided specifically for Black and ethnic minority students. The access course should be followed up with tutor and mentor support in the first year of ITT.

x. **Accommodation** is identified by significant number of students as a source of racism. HEIs need to ensure that their EO policy deals with issues of residential accommodation. Independent accommodation is more difficult to monitor but local residents who offer it should be advised by the ITTI of the law regarding racial discrimination and harassment (Race Relations Act, 1976).

xi. **School placement**, as this book confirms, created particularly acute problems for Black and ethnic minority students. This is a difficult time for all students, especially early in the practice, and if it is not to be a negative experience for this group of students in particular, schools, with the support of the ITTI, need to take the following steps:

- Schools should have an equal opportunities policy in place, that is widely circulated. Copies should be given to all students on placement and to the relevant staff in the ITT institution

- Schools should have copies of the ITTI's EO policy and the management and the teacher/mentors should be familiar with its contents

- Schools with exclusively white teaching staffs should be avoided: it is unreasonable to expect a student on placement to become the school's 'Black experience'

- School and university staff should take responsibility for dealing with any incidents of racism. It should not be left to the student to deal with racism when it occurs. The institutions should set up clear complaints procedures for students who are discriminated against, with a panel that includes members of local RECs or the CRE.

To summarise, the ITTI and its placement schools need to have strong, active, effective and established equal opportunity and anti-racist policies in place and to 'practice what they preach' in every aspect of their work in initial teacher training. In this way the confidence of the students and their place in the institution and the professions will become secure, and then recruitment and success will not require special initiatives and interventionist measures but will be normal and expected.

B. The Funding Bodies

The HEFCE initiative is valuable in highlighting some of the difficulties that arise when the projects funded are interventionist, and particularly when they relate to racial equality. It is clear from the paragraphs reprinted on pages 159 and 160, that HEFCE attempted to build in certain conditions, criteria and monitoring requirements.

With hindsight, however, we can see that the conditions, criteria and monitoring specifications were not fully effective in securing the best possible outcomes to the projects. No preconditions can ever be expected wholly to guarantee outcome in funded projects of this nature but we suggest that future funding designed to further racial equality in education could be more tightly controlled as recommended here.

Circular 9/3 Special Initiatives to Encourage Widening Participation HEFCE March 1993

Ethnic Minorities

8. In 1985 the Swann Committee identified a serious shortage of entrants to teacher training from ethnic minority groups. This is a well recognised problem for which no general solution has yet been identified. The successful encouragement of students from ethnic minorities entering teaching would have a significant and long term effect on the education system in general and ethnic minority communities in particular.

9. Bids are, therefore, invited for clearly targeted initiatives by individual institutions which specifically aim to increase the participation of ethnic minorities in teacher education.

Requirements

10. Bids will be restricted to two per institution. Applications for funding should be no longer than 5 pages of A4 including the cover sheet. Each bid should show a timetable for the proposed work

11. All bids must show the total cost of the project plus a detailed breakdown indicating the institution's own resource contribution and showing, where relevant, any gearing effect on current activity.

Institutions should also provide the following information:

b. Ethnic Minorities

i. Details of current related activity.

ii. Evidence of the existing market and arrangements for targeting

iii. Project objectives, mechanisms for monitoring and evaluating success.

iv. The scope for future developments.

v. The possibilities for wider dissemination within the sector.

vi. Successful applicants will be expected to provide a brief interim report and a full final report on the outcomes...

Criteria For Evaluation

13. Proposals will be assessed against the following criteria:

a. The nature and extent of existing provision and its proven success.

b. The extent to which the project will improve and increase existing provision.

c. The arrangements for monitoring past success and how these arrangements will be extended to the proposed project.

d. The extent of any gearing effect.

e. The scope for wider dissemination.

f. The scope for future development.

---

and from **Circular 22/93: Special Initiatives to Encourage Widening Participation: Funded Projects HEFCE July 1993**, the section on **Monitoring**:

10. With all policy initiatives of this kind. where the Council is using specifically identified funding to support particular objectives, the Council will wish to monitor the effectiveness of the initiatives.

11. Successful institutions are, therefore, required to submit to the Council a project report in September 1994. The report should cover the following areas:

- objectives of the project
- scope of the project
- monitoring procedures used
- extent to which objectives were met
- extent to which dissemination was achieved
- future plans for work directly arising from the project .

12. The reports will be used to identify areas of good practice and indicate to the Council where funding has achieved the maximum benefit.

13. The dissemination of good practice was a key feature of the special initiatives. Institutions are, therefore, requested to make available any materials and information arising from the initiative to all HE institutions and, in particular, to co-operate with institutions with projects of a similar nature to their own or with those serving similar groups. The Council will be considering further how best to facilitate this — for example through a conference.

The major failure appears to be the short-termism many of the projects. For certain HEIs that bid successfully the HEFCE funding was a stone thrown into a pond: there was a year-long ripple effect and then the institution became just as before. To institutionalise positive change, we make the following recommendations:

1. Conditions

i.   **Time-scale** needs to be realistic. Fewer projects funded for a three year minimum supported and externally monitored throughout — would, on the evidence before us, have had more enduring results.

ii.   The time-scale should be determined by the funding body, not by the institution. If changes are considered, all those involved in the project should be involved in the decision.

2. Consultation

iii. Insufficient and inadequate consultation at a range of different levels appears to have undermined several projects. There is evidence of staff in certain of the ITTIs making arbitrary decisions about whom to target in their project. The subjects targeted should be clearly identified in the submission.

iv.   Members of steering groups and internal committees should fulfil their obligations to attend the meetings.

v.   Meetings should, in some cases, be attended also by members of the funding body or the external evaluators.

vi.   Researchers and project workers should attend the meetings of the steering group and/or receive minutes.

vii. Students should be entitled to attend certain steering group meetings by prior arrangement.

viii. Provision should be made for all the students involved in the projects to be informed about the stated objectives and also the development and progress of the project.

ix.   There should be a written code of practice setting out the role of the steering committee, the ITTI management, the project leader, the project workers and the students in the project. This code of practice should be given to everyone in the institution who is involved in the project and to the headteachers, the governing body and the class teachers and mentors in the teaching placement schools. It should also be conspicuously displayed and copies should be made available on request to all students in the ITTI.

3. Project staff

x.   Staff employed on short-term contracts from outside of an institution are disadvantaged in a range of ways. Their very presence can invite suspicion and anxiety and their ignorance of the culture and hidden agenda of the institution make them vulnerable to exclusion. If a decision is made, as in a substantial number of these projects, to employ Black/ethnic minority staff as temporary workers in (in some cases) a white-only (and in every case, of course, white-dominated) institution under an established member of staff who is white, problems are virtually inevitable. We suggest that alternative structures be sought.

xi.   The status of the specially-appointed staff needs to be high. Their presence needs to announced and explained. The funding body should be clear that institutions do not leave the project workers to explain their presence themselves. In two of the six projects reported here and, on anecdotal evidence, in several others, the project workers found themselves constantly being taken for students.

xii.   Marginalisation of the project workers inhibited their work considerably. Access to the information they required was in the gift of the institutions' staff. Funding bodies need to make it a condition for host institutions to supply the steering group and project workers promptly with relevant steering information about the institution and about the students targeted in the project.

4. Criteria for Grants

xiii.   The criteria for evaluation, reprinted above from HEFCE Circular 9/3, need to extended in a number of ways, to prevent the embedding of projects into unsuitable host institutions. The foremost criterion must be that the institution already has an equal opportunities policy in place and can demonstrate evidence of

a) its wide dissemination and high profile in the institution

b) its implementation

c) the members of staff, to include management staff, accountable for its implementation and answerable to the policy.

xiv. The institution should be required to indicate how it will guarantee high status for any staff funded by the external funding body.

xv. The institution should not place any students in schools for their teaching practice that do not have an equal opportunities policy and code of practice and cannot name a member of staff with responsibility for equal opportunities in the school. It should be a criterion that Black/ethnic minority students are apprised of the policies and staff responsible for their implementation, in the ITTI and the school.

5. Monitoring and evaluation

xvii. An independent evaluator or team of evaluators should be appointed at the start by the Funding Body.

xviii. They should be consulted in the process of selecting from the bids submitted and be expected to visit the institutions during the project and to attend at least two steering committee meetings.

xix. Institutions should be required to monitor outcomes — e.g. of recruitment — for three years following the completion of the project.

xx. The outcomes should be two-fold: a high success rate among the subjects of the project and evidence of a more open and equal-based institution with a greater proportion of Black/ethnic minority students on roll in the future.

The Funding Body then, needs to be aware of the 'vicious circle' that can operate in education against Black and ethnic minority people and to direct their funding at breaking this circle. The vicious circle operates at every level, as these projects have revealed:

Where all the staff were white, students in schools found themselves to be the school's 'Black experience' and to be the targets of racism. The students were in no doubt that the presence of Black/ethnic minority teachers would have alleviated or even prevented this situation.

This dearth of Black teachers leads to a dearth of Black people in HE and specifically in ITT. This serves to marginalise and isolate further the students we are trying to support so that they can complete their studies, become teachers, and so break the vicious circle.

At present, interventionist strategies are too short-term and are not always followed through. As long as all monitoring of institutions ends with the cessation of these short-term projects, the law of inertia will obtain and the institutions may revert to their former character. As this book demonstrates it is in HEIs that have revised their policy staffing and intake and thus their culture, that projects will be most successful. It is the failure rate in those which are not required to change themselves that should be of foremost concern to the funding bodies and to the education system overall.

Index

academic objectivity 13, 17, 28
access 97, 113, 114, 152, 154, 157
accommodation of Black student
teachers 72, 73, 167
accreditation of prior learning 153,
154
achievement 24, 68, 117, 119
admissions 89, 114, 115, 121, 132,
153, 154
anti-racism 19, 101, 103, 114, 118

bilingual students 2, 116, 121, 122,
138, 148, 158, 160
see *also* language
bilingual teachers 135, 152, 160

careers guidance 37, 51, 91, 92, 134,
141, 148
counselling 55, 64, 94, 95, 157, 166

equal opportunities policy and
practice 77, 83, 103, 123, 148,
165, 168, 172
ethnic monitoring 63, 64, 114, 115,
116, 131, 167
exclusion 60

financial hardship 63, 73

gender 16, 101, 122, 155, 166

HEFCE 1, 2, 3, 29, 35, 61, 71, 97,
165, 168, 169, 170, 172

induction 3, 156
IQ 14, 15

language 3, 5, 116-124

management 5, 29, 149, 157, 159,
162, 172
mentoring 4, 97-111, 144, 145, 148,
156, 160, 166, 167
monitoring progression 3, 98, 148,
161, 173

national curriculum 61, 64, 74, 142,
158

parents 37, 50, 94, 109, 159
positive action 90, 96, 134, 138, 144,
167

racial discrimination 53, 64, 66, 81,
155, 161, 164
racial harassment 75, 77, 98
racism 16, 18, 21, 23, 25, 31, 38, 41,
46, 49, 64, 68, 74, 75, 79, 82, 91
103, 132, 149, 159, 160, 168, 173
recruitment 3, 49, 54, 66, 89, 113,
129, 151, 166
research 13, 16-29, 31-33
role models 38, 46, 51, 53, 103, 106,
141, 151, 163

school placement 64, 65, 67, 72, 80,
81, 104, 148, 159, 160, 167
school students 23, 24, 36, 37, 41,
49, 51, 60, 78, 130, 131, 132, 137
scientific racism 14-17
staff development in HEIs 30, 148,
149, 150, 165, 166, 168
stereotyping 20, 21, 22, 26, 31, 32,
60, 67, 68, 82, 148

teacher expectations 16, 17, 23, 25,
60, 67, 76, 78, 93
teachers, Black and ethnic minority
36, 38, 43, 45, 46, 47, 132, 133,
138-141, 151
time-scale 62, 136, 163, 171, 174
tokenism 5, 72, 163, 173